D0422055

YOUR LIFE IS YOUR MESSAGE

Once, while Mahatma Gandhi's train was pulling slowly out of the station, a European reporter ran up to his compartment window. "Do you have a message I can take back to my people?" he asked. It was Gandhi's day of silence, a vital respite from his demanding speaking schedule, so he didn't reply. Instead, he scrawled a few words on a scrap of paper and passed it to the reporter: "My life is my message."

YOUR LIFE
IS YOUR
MESSAGE

Finding Harmony with Yourself,
Others, and the Earth

EKNATH EASWARAN

NEW YORK

Copyright © 1992 The Blue Mountain Center of Meditation

Previously published by Nilgiri Press.

Library of Congress Cataloging-in-Publication Data

Easwaran, Eknath.
    Your life is your message : finding harmony with yourself, others, and the earth / by Eknath Easwaran.—1st ed.
        p. cm.
    ISBN 0-7868-6220-3
        1. Meditations. I. Title.
BL624.2.E38   1996
291.4—dc20   95-46095
            CIP

First Hyperion Edition
10 9 8 7 6 5 4 3 2 1

Table of Contents

PART THREE
FINDING HARMONY WITH THE EARTH

Your Life Is Your Message

CONSERVATION BIOLOGISTS call the elephant a "keystone" species. Just as an arch cannot stand without its keystone, many other species, and sometimes entire ecosystems, would be lost without the elephant. On the African savannah, the elephant's foraging creates a mixture of woodlands and grasslands, making the savannah hospitable to many more creatures, from the zebra to the giraffe to the baboon. In drier climates, it provides water not only for itself but for all the other species by creating new water holes and even digging wells. Because of the elephant, a huge, hungry animal with gentle habits, the entire ecosystem flourishes.

I believe that we human beings are meant for no less a role. Today, because of our skills and technology, human society has assumed the position of keystone in the vast, delicately balanced arch of nature. Like the elephants in the forest, our lives affect all the other creatures, plants, and elements around us. They all depend upon us for support and protection.

In one way, our influence now is far from benign. Rather than supporting the rest of life, human beings often seem to be at odds with it. Scientists tell us that many of our social and business activities are not only driving other species to extinction but are threatening the water, soil, and atmosphere on which our own lives depend. We seem to have trouble relating even to our own species. The tension and alienation of our inner cities, the increase in poverty and homelessness, the drug abuse and high suicide rate among our young people all suggest that we lack the wisdom to protect ourselves, let alone the rest of nature.

Yet in another sense, there is great promise today. Around the world – even in some of the countries most troubled by poverty or civil war or pollution – many thoughtful people are making a deep, concerted search for a way to live in harmony with each other and the earth. Their efforts, which rarely reach the headlines, are among the most important events occurring today. Sometimes these people call themselves peace workers, at other times environmentalists, but most of the time they work in humble anonymity. They are simply quiet people changing the world by changing themselves.

The purpose of this book is to encourage those people and the changes they are making. In it, I hope to underscore the tremendous potential of such "tremendous trifles," to use G. K. Chesterton's phrase, for improving our lives and the world we live in, and I will be offering some practical suggestions on how to make those changes more satisfying and more powerful.

Through such unobtrusive, almost inaudible work, the changes we would like to see in the world around us can begin immediately in our own lives, making us more secure, more contented, and more effective. Each of us has the capacity to become a little keystone, a healing and protecting force in the family, with friends, at work, in the community, in the environment.

Such little changes can seem painfully small when compared to the kinds of crises we read about in the headlines, but through my personal experience I have become convinced that there is no instrument of change more powerful than the well-lived life. Having had the privilege of growing up in Mahatma Gandhi's India, walking with him, studying his life, and trying to live by his example, I can say that his simple, loving life has done more to benefit the world than all the speeches and policies composed by politicians in this century – however eloquent, however well-meaning.

Once, while Mahatma Gandhi's train was pulling slowly out of the station, a reporter ran up to him and asked for a message to take back to his people. Gandhi's reply was a hurried line scrawled on a scrap of paper: "My life is my message."

This is the message which all our children are waiting and hoping for. In the coming decades they face the daunting prospect of inheriting our world, with its debts, its national antagonisms, its injured environment. What they are often trying to express through anger or rebellion is a need to be loved – not through words or gifts, but through our personal example. "Say it with flowers" is not enough. We need to say it with our lives. How else will they know that living in harmony with each other and the earth is possible?

Taken together, these small daily efforts to improve our ordinary lives add up to a very powerful force that, in the years to come, can become a kind of spiritual revolution, providing a firm foundation for the kind of political, economic, and ecological improvements we need to make.

In the past two centuries, the world has seen several revolutions. Some of them have brought salutary changes, while others have brought only suffering, but I would venture to say that none of them has brought us the peace our minds are hungering for or the love our hearts are thirsting for. Without such a spiritual foundation, I don't think any political or economic policy, however new, however brilliant, can fill the crying needs of humanity or protect the earth from the pressure those unfilled needs exert on it.

What I am referring to goes well beyond what we normally call social change. While I have the deepest respect for all those working selflessly to serve the world, many of the so-called "reformers" I have seen both in India and this country have an unpromising approach. They look down from the soapbox or pulpit and say, "Let me reform you, Diane, and you, Steve, and of course you, Bob."

If Bob says, "What about you?" they reply, "Oh, that can wait. Let me start with Diane and Steve and you."

That is a familiar refrain in international politics, international economics, international aid, even international education. But the great spiritual teachers of all religions – men and women who have devoted their lives to the art of living in complete harmony, like Francis of Assisi, Teresa of Avila, the Compassionate Buddha, Mahatma Gandhi – say, "Oh no! You start with yourself." There is not much purpose served by preaching to others or by talking at them. The only way to influence people for the better – your family, your friends, your club, your class, your clinic, your society, even your enemies – is through your personal example. Harmony with the environment – the alleviation of our environmental crisis – and harmony with others – the easing of our social, political, and economic difficulties – both begin with a third harmony: harmony with ourselves.

Even though they may not realize it consciously, people

absorb something deep below the conscious level when they see a man who is at peace with himself, a woman who finds her happiness in making life a little better for the community. It is the same mental dynamic as advertisers use in their roadside billboards. While you are traveling on the freeway, you may not notice the billboards consciously, but a certain part of their message seeps into the unconscious, and influences you the next time you go to the store.

Similarly, when you are able to live with joy, giving your time and energy to improving the quality of life for all, you are not only fulfilling your highest destiny, you are also helping all those around you to grow to their full height. As you will see from the challenges outlined in this book, this is not an easy path. Self-transformation is arduous work, especially at first; but each tiny change brings with it the joyful awareness that your life is gradually becoming a force for peaceful change.

Nothing is more important today. Much effort is going into the search for substitutes for environmentally harmful products, like the chlorofluorocarbons which damage the ozone layer or the chemicals which pollute our groundwater, but what we need just as urgently is a substitute for the real culprit – a way of life which demands ever-increasing amounts of material resources while providing ever-decreasing satisfaction. To replace it, we need more than just a plan for efficient energy use or designs for solar-powered cars, although these are always welcome. We need a way of life which gives back more than it takes, enhancing the world around us rather than exploiting and polluting it. So, while the chemists search for substitutes for CFCs and the engineers seek to make solar and wind power profitable, the environmental crisis is challenging us all to undertake an even more important search: the search for a sustainable, fully satisfying way of life, based not on exploiting the external environment, but on taking full advantage of the riches inside us – the nobility, compassion, and desire for peace that lie hidden in every heart. This is not work that can be done for us by corporations or governments; we each have to do it ourselves.

Yet we do not have to do it alone. My grandmother, who was my spiritual teacher, always used the tamarind tree to illustrate the power of ordinary people. The tamarind is a big tree, with very small, thin leaves. On a hot day, the people of my old state of Kerala like to sleep in its shade. The leaves are so numerous and are packed so close together that they protect us from the tropical sun just as if they were one large canopy. "Little Lamp, you don't have to look for big people," Granny would tell me. "Look for little people like yourself, then band together and work together in harmony."

So don't be intimidated by position or power or wealth. If little people like you and me work together, we can do a great deal to transform the world.

Reading This Book

THIS BOOK IS meant as a companion for
a gradual process of self-transformation, in which you can
find and establish harmony with yourself, with the people
around you, and with the earth. In it, I have tried to give
short glimpses of a way of life both inwardly fulfilling
and outwardly beneficial. Read these little pieces straight
through or in any order that follows your needs. Come
back to them as often as you like. Like flower seeds
which reveal their true beauty only after they are planted
and watered, the simple but profound truths of the world's
great spiritual heritage will release their transformative
power only when you plant them in your heart through
deep concentration and reflection.

For this reason, throughout the book, I often refer to a
simple Eight-Point Program of spiritual growth which I
have used myself and taught for over thirty years. The eight
daily practices it comprises are distilled from the mystical
tradition sometimes called the Perennial Philosophy, which
has found expression within all the major religious traditions of the world: Hindu, Jain, and Buddhist; Islamic and
Zoroastrian; Jewish and Christian. They embody millennia
of experience in the art of absorbing spiritual wisdom and
making it an integral part of daily life.

In my Eight-Point Program, I have adapted these traditional practices to the demands and opportunities of an
active modern life. They can be used by all those who want
to enrich their life by harnessing their deepest reserves
of creativity and compassion. The program requires no

particular religious beliefs, and can be practiced fully within your own religious context, or even if you are allergic to all religious dogma.

Basic instructions in the eight points, which I have discussed at length in my other books, are contained in the text of this book. A list of the eight points and an index for them is included on page 124.

PART ONE

Finding Harmony with
Yourself

Shedding an Old Skin

DURING THE MONSOON time in Kerala, the state in South India from which I come, the paddy fields stretch like an endless emerald carpet towards the horizon. It is a time of great growth and joy for all creatures. As a little boy, I used to walk beside my spiritual teacher, my mother's mother, across those rice fields to our ancestral temple.

As we walked, I would often see the cast-off skin of a snake, lying like a lace ribbon beside the path. One day, I asked Granny, "Why do these snakes have to lose their skin?" Her reply was full of wisdom. I realize now that she was speaking of more than snakes. "If snakes do not shed their skin," she replied, "they cannot grow. They will suffocate in their old skin." I often remember her words. Today we too need to grow. The intense restlessness of our young people, the dissatisfaction and stifled idealism which haunts so many older people – these are signs that our society is ready to shed an outworn definition of who we are and what we can become. While I appreciate the attempts made by governments and distinguished groups and some corporations to solve our environmental or social problems, the solution lies ultimately in your hands and mine. What kind of image do we have of ourselves? What is our purpose in living?

By undertaking to answer those questions from our own experience, we will be laying the foundations of a truly sustainable society.

The Pauper Becomes a Prince

JUST AS THERE is one kind of hunger in
the Third World – the need for food and clothes and medi-
cal care – similarly in advanced Western countries like ours
there is a gnawing hunger for fulfillment, which is not
appeased by possessions or power or fame. Within each
of us there is an undeniable demand for a joy that does not
come and go, for a sense of purpose, for knowing who we
are. The Compassionate Buddha would say that below the
surface level of consciousness, we are all being haunted by
this hunger. Without a way to dive below the surface and
answer the questions "Who am I?" and "Where can I find
a joy that lasts?" we will never be quite content.

Yet it is possible to travel slowly but surely into the
depths of the unconscious and there transform our personality. We can actually make a new person of ourselves; we
can become the kind of person we dream of being. Meister
Eckhart calls this the pauper becoming the prince.

Patanjali, a teacher of meditation in ancient India, called
meditation Raja Yoga. Raja, of course, means "king"; so
raja yoga is those disciplines which have come down in
all the great religions through which men and women born
commoners become royalty, with a crown on their heads
and a scepter in their hands. If you ask them, "What is your
kingdom?" they will answer with quiet, unshakable con-
fidence, "We rule the country of our mind and the kingdom
of our life." George Bernard Shaw put it in his inimitable
style: "To be in hell is to drift: to be in heaven is to steer."

Unless and until we have some measure of sovereignty over our thinking process, lasting fulfillment will be beyond our reach.

The Little Musk Deer

IN THE INDIAN TRADITION they tell a story which describes the spiritual search very well. It is about the musk deer, a gentle creature which makes its home on the lower slopes of the Himalayas. One day, it is said, a little musk deer went to his granny musk deer. He was puzzled. "Granny," he said, "I smell a haunting fragrance. What is it? Where is it coming from?" "Why don't you go and smell the animals in the forest to see if it comes from any of them," said his granny. So the musk deer went to the lion, smelled the lion, and said, "No, it's not the lion." Then he went to the tiger and said, "Oh no, it's definitely not the tiger." Then the monkey, then the bear, then the fish, then the elephant; one by one, he went to all the animals in the forest and finally, quite baffled, returned to Granny. "I have been to every animal in the forest," he said, "and none of them has this perfume." Granny just smiled wisely and said, "Then here, smell your own paw." The musk deer lifted his paw, gave it a sniff, and let out a cry of joy.

"It comes from me," he cried. "It comes from me! It comes from me!"

FROM THE EIGHT-POINT PROGRAM:
Meditation

THE HEART OF MY Eight-Point Program
is meditation: half an hour every morning, as early as is
convenient. Do not increase this period; if you want to
meditate more, have half an hour in the evening also.

If you can, it is a good idea to set aside a room in your
home to be used only for meditation and spiritual reading.
After a while that room will become associated with meditation in your mind, so that simply entering it will have a
calming effect. If you cannot spare a room, have a particular corner. Whichever you choose, keep your meditation
place clean, well ventilated, and reasonably austere.

Sit in a straight-backed chair or on the floor and gently
close your eyes. If you sit on the floor, you may need to
support your back lightly against a wall. You should be
comfortable enough to forget your body, but not so comfortable that you become drowsy.

Whatever position you choose, be sure to keep your
head, neck, and spinal column erect in a straight line. As
concentration deepens, the nervous system relaxes and you
may begin to fall asleep. It is important to resist this tendency right from the beginning, by drawing yourself up
and away from your back support until the wave of sleep
has passed.

Once you have closed your eyes, begin to go *slowly,* in
your mind, through a passage from the scriptures or the
great mystics which you have memorized for use in meditation. I usually recommend the Prayer of St. Francis of
Assisi to begin with:

Lord, make me an instrument of thy peace.
Where there is hatred, let me sow love;
Where there is injury, pardon;
Where there is doubt, faith;
Where there is despair, hope;
Where there is darkness, light;
Where there is sadness, joy.

O Divine Master, grant that I may not so much seek
To be consoled as to console,
To be understood as to understand,
To be loved as to love;
For it is in giving that we receive,
It is in pardoning that we are pardoned,
It is in dying [to self] that we are born to eternal life.

Do not follow any association of ideas or try to think about the passage. If you are giving your attention to each word, the meaning cannot help sinking in. When distractions come, do not resist them, but give more attention to the words of the passage. If your mind strays from the passage entirely, bring it back gently to the beginning and start again.

When you reach the end of the passage, you may use it again as necessary to complete your period of meditation until you have memorized others. It is helpful to have a wide variety of passages for meditation, drawn from the world's major traditions. Each passage should be positive and practical, drawn from a major scripture or from a mystic of the highest stature.

The secret of meditation is simple: we become what we meditate on. When you use the Prayer of St. Francis every day in meditation, you are driving the words deep into your consciousness. Eventually they become an integral part of your personality, which means that they will be an active force in your life, sowing good will in your thoughts, your relationships, and in all your actions.

Nature with a Capital N

WHEN MY WIFE and I were living with my mother on the Blue Mountain in India, we came to know a European couple who lived nearby. They were always very hospitable to us, but the husband had an aversion to the word "God." Whenever I said "God", he would correct me: "Nature with a capital N." This did not bother me at all, since in India's five-thousand-year-old tradition there are many authorities who state that God has countless different names, while there are just as many who say that the ultimate reality is not He or She but It, and has no name at all. So when my friend would greet me and ask me how my mother was, I would answer, "Very well, thank you, thanks to the grace of nature with a capital N."

When I was first in Berkeley, I discovered that America has its share of individualists as well. There were occasions at Christmastime when I would say, "Hey, Tom, have a Merry Christmas," and Tom would say, "I don't believe in Christianity." Then I would say, "Happy Hanukkah!" and he would say, "I don't believe in Judaism either." So I would just say, "Have a nice day!"

None of these things makes any difference. In order to lead the spiritual life and practice meditation, you don't have to belong to any particular religion, or any religion at all. When I talk about the Self, or what the traditional religions call God, I am not talking about somebody outside of you, swinging in a heavenly hammock between the Milky Way and Andromeda galaxies. I am talking about someone who is inside of you all the time – the resident of your deepest consciousness, who is waiting to be discovered, calling out to be courted. As Meister Eckhart says, "God is in, we are out; God is at home, we are abroad."

Turning Inward

ONE OF THE MANY Hindu names for God is Krishna, which is derived from the Sanskrit root *krish,* "to draw or attract." It is a poetic way of implying that the Self, by whatever name we call him or her, is drawing us all the time from the depths of our own consciousness. Because of our conditioning, we think this call is coming from outside of ourselves. So, for a time, we act as if security could be found on the beach at Saint-Tropez, or in a bright red sports car, or in a fashionable boutique on Rodeo Drive.

I have many friends, both in India and America, who have made millions or become famous. I have asked some of them whether they found what they were looking for. Those with some self-knowledge have told me in a whisper, "No, what I was looking for escaped through my fingers." Everybody, even if they are not aware of it, is

seeking this same radiant personality which is always living in you and me. Even if we have committed mistakes,
the Self doesn't relocate himself. Even if we have caused
endless trouble to ourselves and others, the Divine Mother
is still there within us. So in all our work, the first thing to
keep in mind is that the same Self lives within every one of
us and can be discovered. The purpose of meditation is to
make this supreme discovery, which will release into our
lives a flood of love and energy, great wisdom and an
unerring faculty for seeing into the heart of the problems
which face the world today.

A Continuing Source of Joy

*I believe that if one man gains spiritually the
whole world gains with him and, if one man falls,
the whole world falls to that extent.*
                                    – *Mahatma Gandhi*

WE ARE ALL INCLINED to get over-
whelmed at times and to ask, "What can I, one person, do
to right problems like pollution and hunger?" Gandhi's
reply is simple but challenging: you just raise your own
consciousness and you will raise the consciousness of the
entire world. That is what he did.

All of us can give a great gift to the world by looking at
our life and gradually removing from it the things that are
not simple and beautiful. I was terribly touched to see in

the paper yesterday how many people, both old and young, were sleeping through cold winter nights under the bridges and on the pavement in San Francisco. Can you imagine? Even in the richest country on the face of the earth, many people have no place to sleep.

I regard these people as my kith and kin, just as I regard the hungry children of Africa as my own. That is what happens when you begin to be aware that the Self in you is the same as the Self in all these desperate people. When you see this unity, you will find a continuing source of joy in making wise use of your money, your time, your energy, your resources in the service of all.

Inner Simplicity

AS YOUR PRACTICE of meditation deepens, your concentration on the inspirational passage will gradually become so profound that you won't hear the cars on the road or the planes in the sky. You will hardly be aware of your body. This tremendous calm brings many benefits to the body, but even more to the mind. Simplification of your life has started at the deepest level.

As you dive deeper and deeper into your consciousness, you will make the discovery that your needs are not just for your own personal satisfaction and prestige but for enriching the lives of all those around you. You will begin to think as urgently about the needs of others as you've been thinking about your own. With this expansion of consciousness comes a flood of loving energy that transforms your life and the world around you. The idea of buying or doing something for yourself at the expense of others or of the forests or rivers or air becomes unthinkable.

You Are Not What You Wear

I LIKE TO DRESS WELL, and I appreciate it when people try to make the best of their appearance, but I am often surprised when I see some of the bizarre and expensive looks that fashion urges on us, and especially on our young people. When I go to get my hair cut, I usually take a look at the magazines meant for teenagers – *Seventeen* or *Glamour* – and I wish I could add my perspective: there is no one more glamorous or beautiful than the men and women who have discovered their true Self.

In India, we have many stories to illustrate this. When a great sculptor went to sculpt the Buddha's image, he was so dazzled by his splendor that he said, "Your beauty blinds me, Compassionate One. I can't look at you. How am I to make your image?" The Buddha said, "Here, I shall cast my reflection in the water." And so the serene, noble images we now have of the Buddha are said to be taken from only a reflection of his real beauty.

In the Dhammapada, the Buddha, this source of beauty, gives a real beauty secret: You are not the clothes you have worn; you are not the jewelry you have bought. All that you are is the result of what you have thought. Through meditation, you can beautify your thinking and make your personality shine brighter and brighter.

This is a very different concept of beauty from what we see in the media. According to the Buddha, everyone is born to be beautiful – not just for the first twenty-five years, but always. The source of all beauty is within.

The Buddha's Fragrance

THE GIRLS IN CENTRAL India, where I used to teach at a junior college, did not wear expensive perfumes. Instead, they would go to sleep with strands of jasmine flowers wound in their luxuriant black hair. In the morning they would remove the flowers before they came to class, but the haunting fragrance of jasmine clung to their hair and followed them into the classroom.

I'm afraid the young men's thoughts often wandered from my lectures on *Hamlet* and *The Tempest*.

The Buddha uses a very similar image when he tells us that it is possible for ordinary people like us to learn to love not just a few people close to us – our partner, our children, our friends, or even our whole neighborhood – but to become love itself, loving men, women, children, lions, tigers, elephants, dogs, cats, everyone. When you go near such people, says the Buddha, you will find that there is a fragrance surrounding them, which enters your heart almost without your awareness. When you spend time with such a person, you will be plunged into a fragrance that will follow you home and haunt you.

It takes a long, long time, but all of us can develop this

all-embracing, all-consuming love. One great mystic
describes it as a love that will not let you go. Even if you
do not want to love, you can't help it. You couldn't hate
anyone even if you wanted to. You could try to say, "Love,
leave me alone!" but it would simply reply, "No – you're
mine."

Light the Lamp Within

RECENTLY I WENT to a store specifically
for men. I was curious to find out how successful men
spend their time and hard-earned money, what attracts
them, and what they think will enhance their appearance.
At the cosmetics counter, I was given a little pamphlet on
the care of the face. There was a long list of lotions, rinses
to remove the lotions, and enough procedures to take one
full hour every night. From what I could grasp, the makers
of these lotions honestly believe that if you pay such close
attention to your skin you will be loved everywhere.

I don't want to be a wet blanket, but I must point out one
of life's oldest truths. Most people do respond to physical
beauty, but after a time – it can be a painfully short time –
some other well-groomed face may be receiving the attention you used to get.

Age cannot be postponed indefinitely. Whatever
artifical aids we apply, it has to be confessed that once
we get into our thirties – some people say once we get past
twenty-five – the physical scales are tilted against us. On

the other hand, the beauty that comes from a peaceful mind and loving heart actually grows with age. In the case of my spiritual teacher, my grandmother, even in her seventies she took our breath away by the glow of her skin, the gentleness of her eyes. Everyone in the family would gather around her because all were aware that here was beauty and femininity that time could not touch.

If you want to look at the most beautiful eyes in the world, don't look at the cover of Vogue but at a picture of Sri Ramana Maharshi, a sage who was with us in India until 1950, and who was the original of the spiritual teacher in Somerset Maugham's famous novel *The Razor's Edge.* The more you look into his eyes the deeper you will fall into them. There's an old saying that the eyes are the windows of the soul. It is only when you come in contact with such people that you can understand that when the lamp is lit inside, the light shines out through all the windows.

The Second Half of Life

I am the feminine qualities: fame, beauty
perfect speech, memory, intelligence, loyalty,
and forgiveness. — *Bhagavad Gita*

PEOPLE WHO IDENTIFY themselves with
their body often find the latter half of life a great burden.
Only when you learn to identify yourself with the Self will
the latter half of your life become a great blessing.

Once, when a friend and I were walking at the local
shopping district, a young woman reporter stopped me.
She apologized for interrupting my walk and said, "Do
you mind if I ask you a question?" She cleared her throat.
"What would you say is the most unpleasant thing about
growing old?"

I wasn't offended. She was a nice young woman; she
was just reflecting the assumptions which underlie all our
modern attitudes. So I smiled and said, "Now you'd better
take down what I say. The latter part of my life is wonderful. In fact, there is no comparison with the first part. All
the physical vigor and the running about and the – what do
you call it? – the vim and razzle-dazzle of early life, it's all
'sound and fury, signifying nothing.'"

When you have only your physical appearance to
depend on, I might have added if I had known her better,
there is no escape from the ravages of time. That is why
spiritual teachers say, Enjoy your youth, but don't neglect
to light the lamp of beauty inside, which will glow brighter
with the passage of time.

Our society lives by the rather juvenile theory that

beauty and joy are limited to a particular period in life. It's true that children have a marvelous beauty of their own, but every child has to grow up. Teenagers have a certain beauty of their own, but they, too, have to grow up. Similarly, the twenty-somethings and the thirty-somethings will eventually become forty- and fifty-somethings.

When my grandmother, in her sixties, came and sat with us in our ancestral home, she was the center of all attention. Her beauty came entirely from within, a beauty born of the highest feminine qualities. Forgiveness, inward strength, the use of gentle words (which means gentle thoughts), all play a part in making a woman – or a man! – beautiful.

Whatever religion you belong to, whatever country you belong to, everybody responds to this kind of inner beauty. You don't have to advertise. To use one of the great similes from Sri Ramakrishna, you will be like a lotus opening in the rays of the morning sun. The lotus doesn't need to say, "Where are the bees?" The bees are looking for the lotus. All of us, inwardly, are looking for this kind of beauty and love that grows with the passage of time.

Harnessing Anger

JUST AS WE LIVE in an external, physical world, we live at the same time in an internal world of thoughts, feelings, and desires. While our modern civilization has made great strides in understanding the external world and using it for our comfort, we have barely begun to explore the inner world. Only now are we beginning to recognize that the forces in this internal world – forces like anger, greed, and fear – have the power to devastate the mind, despoil the earth, and destroy human beings. We need to learn how these winds blow, how they can be directed, and how they can be put to work. In the countryside where I live, I often see windmills harnessing the power of the wind, pumping water from deep beneath the earth to feed the local dairy cows and irrigate crops.

Windmills put the wind to work. Similarly, through meditation, you can set up an anger mill, which will put your anger to work, drawing the living waters of compassion and creativity from the depths of your heart to help all those around you. Gandhi learned this secret in South Africa. "I have learnt through bitter experience," he wrote, "the one supreme lesson to conserve my anger, and as heat conserved is transmuted into energy, even so our anger controlled can be transmuted into a power which can move the world." Gandhiji is not quoting a book or telling us what his teacher said. He is speaking from his own experience. Harnessing his anger about the indignities that were heaped upon him and others in South Africa, he changed the world.

Repetition of the Mantram

A MANTRAM IS A powerful spiritual
formula which, when repeated silently in the mind, has
the capacity to transform consciousness. There is nothing
magical about this. It is simply a matter of practice, as all
of us can verify for ourselves.

Every religious tradition has a mantram, often more
than one. For Christians the name of Jesus itself is a
powerful mantram; Catholics also use *Hail Mary* or *Ave
Maria*. Jews may use *Barukh attah Adonai*, 'Blessed art
thou, O Lord,' or the Hasidic formula *Ribono shel olam*,
'Lord of the universe.' Muslims repeat the name of Allah
or *Allahu akbar*, 'God is great.' Probably the oldest
Buddhist mantram is *Om mani padme hum*, referring to
the 'jewel in the lotus of the heart.' In Hinduism, among
many choices, I recommend *Rama*, which was Mahatma
Gandhi's mantram.

Select a mantram that appeals to you deeply. Then, once
you have chosen, do not change your mantram. Otherwise,
as the nineteenth-century Indian mystic Sri Ramakrishna
puts it, you will be like a person digging shallow wells in
many places; you will never go deep enough to find water.

Repeat your mantram silently whenever you get
the chance: while walking, while waiting, while doing
mechanical chores like washing dishes, and especially
when you are falling asleep.

You will find that this is not mindless repetition; the
mantram will help to keep you relaxed and alert. Whenever

you are angry or afraid, nervous or worried or resentful, repeat the mantram until the agitation subsides. The mantram works to steady the mind, and all these emotions are power running against you which the mantram can harness and put to work.

The Space Between Thoughts

IN THE BUDDHA'S representation of the thinking process, thoughts are like monkeys getting ahold of each other's tails. Each thought is separate, but because of the speed with which thought travels, a series of thoughts appears as one unbroken line.

That's what we call anger. Anger is not one thought but a large number of angry thoughts – "I hate her, I hate her, drop dead, drop dead" – repeated a hundred times until they look like one long, sinister crocodile. As long as your thinking is speeded up, there is no way to escape from this crocodile. So what you try to do through meditation and repeating the mantram is to slow down your thoughts until you begin to see a little light between one "drop dead" and the next – just a little beam of light.

Seeing this space between thoughts is the first step towards realizing that you don't have to be anger's plaything. As you slow down the mind, you will learn to step between two angry thoughts, separating two tremendous mental forces like a kind of Charles Atlas, and say, "That's it, boys; break it up! Shake hands and go home. I don't want to see you here again."

It's going to be hard, but you can keep them apart. After you've learned this skill, you may still get angry (there will always be others to provoke you just as you will be there to provoke them), but anger will no longer be able to drive you into harsh action or cloud your judgment. All the energy that would have gone into fighting and resentment can now go into compassion and loving action. You will be a healing force wherever you go.

Living to Be One Hundred and Twenty

IN ORDER TO LIVE in harmony with our-selves, others, and the environment, it is important to under-stand the laws of mental dynamics. These inner forces and their effects on our external world have been studied in detail by many of the world's great mystics, who have cast off the spell of separateness and awakened to the unity of all life; the ancient sages of India have especially studied how the mind can influence the body.

One of the sages' surprisingly prescient theories starts with the hypothesis that there is a fixed number of times the heart is meant to beat each year; the number they gave was forty million. While there may be some argument about the precise number, I think it is not too hard to agree that the heart, like any sturdy pump, has a limited working span.

Now here is the brilliant touch, which is close to certain areas of modern heart research. Positive emotions, the

sages say, are always slower and less stressful than negative ones. You can observe it in yourself. The next time you
are getting angrier and angrier and are about to "blow your
top," check your pulse and breathing rhythm. They have
all speeded up. The entire physiological system has been
thrown into overdrive.

In modern heart research, doctors speak of Type A
personalities, of people with "high-risk factors" like a tendency toward anger or competitiveness, leading to high
blood pressure and an increased risk of heart disease. The
sages of ancient India used a different vocabulary, but the
message is similar: when we are frequently angry or afraid
or agitated, they say, our forty million beats last only about
ten months, instead of twelve. We have lost two months of
our life.

On the bright side, the sages give some practical
advice which accords with recent suggestions by respected
researchers in the fields of heart disease and psycho-
neuroimmunology: if you can be patient under attack,
not retaliating but not retreating either, if you can learn to
return good will for ill will and even help those who are
unkind to you, then your forty million beats, instead of
lasting for twelve months, will last for fourteen. You have
gained two months of life. By the sages' calculations, living for the benefit of others should enable us to live to a
full span of one hundred and twenty years of active, loving
service to the world.

Patroling the Mind

I TRY TO FOLLOW in Mahatma Gandhi's footsteps by obeying all just laws very scrupulously. For example, whenever I travel with friends, we keep under the speed limit of fifty-five miles per hour. Partly we do this to reduce global warming, since fifty-five is the most efficient speed for most cars, but we also do it out of a sense of truth – the law is meant to help us, so we like to obey it.

One day, we found ourselves driving at a time when everyone was going at least sixty-five miles per hour – in front of us, in back, and alongside – so we too had to speed up to sixty-five. Then we saw something unusual. A highway patrol car came weaving in and out of the lanes. He didn't stop or arrest anybody; he just wove in and out. In two minutes everybody was back to fifty-five. I enjoyed seeing how quick people's responses are where the highway patrol is concerned. Everybody slowed down – even the most rebellious teenagers on weekend binges.

That's what the mantram does when you start using it on the mind's highway. When your thoughts start racing along at sixty-five, seventy, eighty, in comes the mantram, with lights flashing, weaving between anger and greed and jealousy and malice. All the thoughts slow down. When this happens, you can redirect your negative emotions into positive channels of work for the benefit of the environment and those around you. Eventually, through regular practice, the gala day will come when you can say to anger or insecurity, "Pull over to the side of the road!" And then you can just leave them there.

Changing Gears

THE GOAL OF ALL spiritual disciplines is gradually to bring the mind to a perfect stillness. In automotive terms, you are downshifting from overdrive to top gear, then to second, then finally to neutral. When you develop the capacity to put your mind into neutral, you will have acquired inexhaustible patience. You will be able to listen to another person's point of view with such concentration and detachment – even when your opinions are being torn to shreds – that sometimes you will say to yourself, "Hey, he is right. I am wrong. I can learn from him." That attitude of open-mindedness, of having a slow-going mind which listens very carefully to opposing points of view and is prepared to learn from them, is the beginning of kindness, and kindness is the foundation of a harmonious world. Hurry is unkindness.

Whenever you sit down for meditation, you might remind yourself that you are slowly changing gears, from the fastest to the slowest, until after many years you park your mind, just as you park your car.

At that point, all your energy is saved. Normally, even when we are not consciously acting or speaking, the mind goes on thinking, consuming precious energy. When you have learned to park your mind, a great deal of energy and vitality is saved, strengthening your immune system and vital organs, and lengthening your life.

Slowing Down

SLOWING DOWN is an important spiritual discipline, especially in our speeded-up modern living and working contexts. Hurry makes for tension, insecurity, inefficiency, and superficial living. To guard against hurrying through the day, start the day early and simplify your life so that you do not try to fill your time with more than you can do. When you find yourself beginning to speed up, repeat your mantram to help you slow down.

It is important here not to confuse slowness with sloth, which breeds carelessness, procrastination, and general inefficiency. In slowing down we should attend meticulously to details, giving our very best even to the smallest undertaking.

Parking the Mind in Kindness

A GREAT BONUS that comes when the mind slows down over a long period is that you become a stranger to insecurity and depression. When the mind is going fast, depression is always with you, riding along in the back seat. Where the mind is going slow, enabling you to choose freely which thoughts you think, depression is outside, hitchhiking. You just say, "Sorry, no room," and drive right by.

I am not talking about morality but dynamics. When your car is going fast, you cannot turn or stop. That is a perfect image of the speeded-up mind as it heads for a crash – whether it is rushing in anger, or fear, or greed.

If you want to park your car in the city, you have to get off the freeway, slow down gradually from sixty miles per hour to forty to twenty to a complete halt, then carefully shift into reverse and perform that amazing feat called parallel parking. Similarly, in order to live in inner freedom, you have to learn how to slow down your mind, bring it to a restorative stillness, and park it anywhere you like – in patience, say, or compassion, or love.

It's an amazing skill. I have a few friends who are very skilled at parking in San Francisco. In places where I see almost no room between two cars, they are able to gracefully slip the car in – even on some of San Francisco's steepest streets. When you can do this with your mind, you will find that nothing can upset you. No matter what happens, you can keep your mind securely parked in kindness and understanding. Even one person who has mastered this skill can begin to transform the community where he or she lives.

Fine-Tuning the Mind

I USED TO HAVE a friend who repaired watches. Whenever I had a problem with my watch, I would bring it to him. He would put a magnifying glass on his eye, open my watch, make a few little adjustments, and hand it back saying, "Now it'll work fine."

As your meditation deepens, you will develop an

extraordinary skill: you will be able to examine the workings of your mind just as my friend looked into my watch. When the watch was going too fast, he wouldn't throw it away. He would open it, loosen a wire or tighten a screw, and then reset the time.

Similarly, after years of intense training, you can, so to speak, take out your mind and open it from the back. You will find it a very interesting spectacle. You will see, to your intense amazement, that the anger or fear or greed that had been driving you faster and faster are only forces, which you can harness and transform. They are not you. Slowly, you begin to know just where the anger or greed are located, and you learn how to transform them into compassion and generosity.

Transforming Greed

WHENEVER THE WORLD'S problems seem overwhelming, remember that you have a vast reservoir of energy and creativity within you, which can provide all the resources you need to make a lasting contribution.

Through meditation you begin to develop a kind of map of your consciousness. You will see where there are pockets of anger or greed, waiting like enemy troops to ambush you. Gradually you will come to the tantalizing awareness that all these negative forces, if you can only win them over to your side, will become your friends. That is how Gandhi brought about such monumental changes.

It was not only anger that he learned to harness. According to his friend Sardar Patel, Gandhi found a tremendous source of beneficial power in greed as well. Patel tells a delightful story about a train journey with Gandhi. At every stop, Gandhi would get off and circulate among the crowd with his begging bowl, collecting for the poorest of India's poor. Jewelry, watches, money – he collected anything. And he collected from everyone – men, women, children, rich, poor. Even the beggars were not exempt from his appeals. As Patel, who couldn't resist pulling Gandhi's leg now and then, and a companion watched this strange, wonderful scene, Patel said, If you want to see a human being consumed by greed, look no further.

That is what I call the magic of transformation. Instead of just being greedy for himself, Gandhi had become greedy for all. He handled millions of rupees without a trace of personal greed. Everything was for his work, nothing for himself. Through meditation and training the senses, you can do this with any negative emotion or self-centered desire. Instead of letting the desire ride on you, you can hop on and ride it wherever you like. You can think of it as a motorcycle. Imagine taking a big desire and, instead of being pushed around by it, jumping on it like a Harley-Davidson, opening the throttle, and roaring off straight toward your goal.

This is what the accomplished meditator can do. He or she will say, What is the satisfaction in being crushed by my desire? What is the satisfaction in getting on your knees, your desire jumping on you and opening the throttle? Defy it! All the desire's power will become yours to use as you like.

It takes a long time to understand this, but afterwards,

when a great desire comes, you will have a choice. If it benefits everybody, go ahead and enjoy it. But if you find it doesn't benefit others or yourself, you won't care what your peer group or Madison Avenue says. You will be able to say "No, I am not going to do it, because this is the energy I need to transform myself and the world around me."

Patience

PATIENCE IS ONE of the most valuable allies in the difficult journey of self-transformation. As St. Francis says, "It is in pardoning that we are pardoned." When you are able to be patient with others, you can be patient with yourself, and that will give you all the inner support you need to persevere and make the changes you want to make in your life. But patience can't be acquired overnight. It's just like building up a muscle. Every day you need to work on it, to push its limits. When people tell me they don't have any patience, I always say, "That's only because you've never pushed it."

Every day I push my patience. Whenever people provoke me or cause me difficulties (which is seldom, but it does happen), I don't get agitated or give up on them or try to be critical. I say to myself, "Here's a chance to extend my patience. Let me bear with him until he falls down, and then help him get up. Let me bear with her until she comes around, and then work with her in harmony." That kind of gritting your teeth and bearing it, establishing your roots deeper and deeper in your consciousness, can bring you, as Gandhi proved, an endurance that no government or corporation or institution can shake.

In Sanskrit, God is called *kshamasagara,* an ocean of patience. Look at all that we are doing to the earth, yet because God is an ocean of patience, when we learn to be patient with ourselves and others, we become humble instruments in his hands, bringing harmony and peace to the world.

Keep Chewing!

WHEN YOU ARE TAKING to meditation and beginning to change your habits, it sometimes looks as if you're having a very thin time. I'm not trying to mislead anyone. This is hard work. In fact my younger students sometimes tell me plaintively, "Life used to be so pleasant for us. Why is it now so . . . so icky?"

I sympathize. When I went through the same thing, I complained about it to my spiritual teacher, my grand-mother. She was a very plainspoken teacher, with none of the euphemism of the intellectual, so she simply led me to a nearby amla tree. The amla is a beautiful tree, a little like the mimosa, with a small fruit. She picked a fruit and said, "Here, take a bite." I started chewing. It was pretty awful.

I said, "I've got to spit it out, Granny. It's sour, bitter, unpleasant." She just said, "Bear with me. Keep chewing for a while." So I went on chewing, and to my surprise the amla fruit began to get sweeter and sweeter.

Similarly, meditation and the allied disciplines require sustained enthusiasm every day – even when it seems icky. Especially when it seems icky! If you keep at it, you will find those same disciplines becoming sweeter and sweeter. When meditation time comes around you will find yourself hungering for the inner peace and calm it brings. The time will even come when you want a double helping.

Proud Humility

There comes a time when an individual becomes irresistible and his action becomes all-pervasive in its effect. This comes when he reduces himself to zero.
— *Mahatma Gandhi*

IF I MAY USE a paradoxical phrase, the mystic is a man of proud humility or a woman of humble pride. "Personally," St. Francis of Assisi would say, "I'm nobody. But," he'll add, "do you know who has come to life in my life? Do you know who lives in my heart?"

Gandhi had the same mixture of pride, ambition, and utter meekness. When he was asked, "Don't you want to be president of India?" he said, "No. I want to make myself zero. But I want my actions to benefit all of mankind."

In my own life, when I was starting out on this path, many of my relatives and friends told me, "You have such capacities, such promise – why do you want to throw it all away? Don't you have any ambition?" If they were to ask me that question today, I would say that I simply was not ambitious before. That is why I was content with being a writer and a teacher of literature. Now, in this country of very ambitious people, I have become one of the most ambitious of all. I believe that you and I, in our own lifetime, can make our streets safe, bring harmony to our homes, simplicity to our lives, and depth to our personal relationships.

So as you begin to simplify your life, if people ask you why you don't have any ambition, please tell them that you are only now learning what ambition is.

Be a Work of Art

GREAT SCRIPTURES like the Bhagavad Gita can be looked upon as artist's manuals. Just as painters study their color and drawing manuals, you can read the Gita or the Sermon on the Mount as a living manual to help you make your life a flawless work of art.

This is truly the supreme art. When your life becomes a work of art, your family will benefit from it every day. Even if you are the only person in the family using these artistic tools, like meditation and the mantram, your partner will benefit, as will your children, your friends, and, interestingly enough, even your enemies.

I have been to few homes where the resident was the greatest artwork. When I entered Gandhi's ashram in central India, close to my university, there was not a single artistic artifact there – not even driftwood. In those days I was very culturally oriented, looking for beauty in all kinds of external objects, but when the cottage door opened, at five in the evening, and a brown, blessed figure came out, I saw the greatest statue I have ever seen in my life. The greatest painting I have ever seen came to life. That's the highest ideal for a human being.

The most difficult of the three harmonies is harmony with oneself. It is the real basis for harmony with others and the environment. I love music, but when somebody tells me about a great symphony they have heard I want to say, "I wish you could listen to the divine symphony I hear when my mind becomes still in the depths of meditation." St. Francis used to say, after he heard that symphony coming from the depths of consciousness, "If it had continued a little more, my life itself would have melted away."

PART TWO

Finding Harmony with Others

Happiness

ONCE I ASKED my teacher, my grandmother, why a certain man in our village never seemed to be happy, even though he had all of life's advantages – he was healthy, he had a fine family and a good job, and he even had a full head of hair. Her reply was simple but profound: "It is not possible for life to make a selfish person happy, whatever temporary satisfactions may come along. But," she added, "life cannot but give you joy if you live for the joy of others."

Living at Life's Center

ONLY A FEW CENTURIES ago bright people all over Europe believed that the sun and stars and planets orbited around the earth. Some of the greatest geniuses in the West – Archimedes, Plato, Aristotle, Dante – were absolutely certain that the earth was the center of the universe. It took one man, Copernicus, to knock the bottom out of this theory.

Today we all learn in kindergarten that the sun, not the earth, is the center of the solar system, and that even the sun is but one among billions in a galaxy that is one among billions. But if we look into the world within, which is as real as the world without, we shall find to our consternation that each of us still believes that we are the center of the world. When we say "I love you," what we usually mean is, "I'll do anything for you, provided you accept that I am the center of the universe and keep a steady orbit around me and my desires."

As a professor and as a teacher of meditation, I have lived around young people for over fifty years, and I have had many opportunities to hear Juliet say to Romeo, "Everything will be wonderful if you just keep going around me, because I am the center of the universe." And Romeo replies, "Sure, honey, as long as you keep going around me, since *I* am the center of the universe." Most of the problems we have in the world today arise because we or our company or our nation live on the circumference of life, trying to make the rest of the world orbit around us.

However, the human mind is a precise instrument which can be trained over the course of many decades to reach the center of life. As you learn gradually to understand the real needs of those around you, you will be not unlike Copernicus discovering for our benefit that the earth is not at the center of the solar system. You will be discovering that the individual ego can never be the center of the universe. It is the Self, dwelling in the hearts of all, who is at the center.

You will begin to understand some of the words that are used by great mystics to describe God. Plotinus, for example, calls God "the One." He doesn't say "Supreme Reality" or the "Clear Light," but simply "the One": "So we always move round the One – if we did not, we should dissolve and cease to exist – but we do not always look towards the One." It is God who is at the center, and this center is in the very depths of your consciousness.

Storm Windows

I HAVE HEARD from my friends on the East Coast and in the Midwest that at the beginning of every winter people are careful to install storm windows. These extra panes of glass protect their houses against the bitter winds blowing down from the Arctic. We do something very similar to protect our minds through the practice of meditation and the allied disciplines, particularly in the discipline I call "putting others first," or trying to think of the needs of others before our own.

Although the mystics are sometimes accused of having an overly sunny opinion of human nature, it is they who are actually the most realistic, even hard-nosed, people about the nature of life. Life, they say, shows no quarter to weak people. Life respects only those who have enough inner strength to withstand its fiercest storms.

The Compassionate Buddha taught that we can acquire this inner strength through training the mind. He used a vivid image: "As rain seeps through an ill-thatched hut, passion will seep through an untrained mind." With his flair for communicating difficult truths in simple terms, he was drawing on an experience familiar to his listeners. When the monsoon rains came, a poorly thatched roof would be no protection against the deluge, and the water would pour right into the hut, turning the floor to mud and bringing cold and sickness to the whole family. Similarly, says the Buddha, a poorly trained mind dominated by thoughts of prestige and personal advantage cannot protect us from a flood of frustration and resentment every time life brings us something we don't like.

By contrast, all of us find it quite comfortable to sit by the fireplace in a sturdy building with a strong roof, even in the fiercest of storms. Outside it may be raining cats and dogs, or even elephants and camels, but inside we are safe and dry. The Buddha promises that we can all find such security and comfort within ourselves: "As rain cannot seep through a well-thatched hut, passion cannot seep through a well-trained mind." When you are established in the practice of meditation, having learned to concentrate not so much on what will benefit you personally as on what will bring benefit to all those around you, then you have installed storm windows on the house of your mind. Outside, it can blow, blow, blow. Inside, you will be safe. Life's misfortunes won't be able to touch your security or your compassion.

FROM THE EIGHT-POINT PROGRAM:
Putting Others First

DWELLING ON OURSELVES builds a
wall between ourselves and others. Those who keep thinking about *their* needs, *their* wants, *their* plans, *their* ideas
cannot help becoming lonely and insecure. The simple but
effective technique I recommend is to learn to put other
people first – beginning within the circle of your family
and friends, where there is already a basis of love on which
to build. When husband and wife try to put each other first,
for example, they are not only moving closer to each other,
they are also removing the barriers of their ego-prison,
which deepens their relationships with everyone else as
well.

Changing Channels in the Mind

OFTEN WHEN I PRESENT the spiritual
discipline of putting others first, someone will raise a
very pertinent question: "Are you asking me to become
a doormat?"

Absolutely not. It's not good to let people walk all over
us – neither for us nor for them. It has to be resisted, but it
can be resisted very tenderly as well as very resolutely.
That is the art of gentle, nonviolent resistance which comes
with the practice of these spiritual disciplines. When some-

body is rude to me (which is seldom), don't think that I am not aware of it. I see the rudeness, but through many years of practice I have learned the art of resisting without retaliating, while not retreating either.

At first this can seem impossible. When someone steps on your toes, it is only natural to be angry and want to lash out against that person. That's when the mantram is your most valuable ally. As soon as you feel angry or resentful, start repeating the mantram. If you can, go out for a fast walk while you repeat it. The rhythm of the mantram will blend with the rhythm of your footsteps, which will calm the rhythm of your breathing, which has a close connection with the rhythm of thinking. It can be a hard battle, but eventually you will find your angry thoughts being replaced by the mantram. You will be able to think clearly and compassionately about the situation, and to come up with a response that not only helps the other person grow but draws you closer together as well.

When you have had some practice, you will be able to use your mantram to change channels in your mind as easily as you change the channels of your television. Several years ago, I was introduced by a friend to a gadget that has since become quite familiar: a TV remote control. I enjoyed very much being able to sit in my chair and, when *Conan the Barbarian* appeared, to press the button and change the channel to Jane Austen's *Pride and Prejudice.*

People who have been brought up in a highly scientific and technological culture will find nothing very miraculous about this. Although there is no visible connection between the remote control and the TV, it works. If I don't want to see Conan or the Terminator or Dracula, I don't have to put up with them. I can just point the remote control and replace them with Elizabeth Bennet or Emma Woodhouse.

It is the same with the mantram. According to the Indian mystics, there are six negative channels in the mind: lust, anger, greed, arrogance, infatuation, and malice. For every negative channel, there is also a positive channel. When you see anger appearing on the screen in his bearskin, waving a club and urging you to retaliate, you can pull out your mantram and switch the channel to compassion and understanding. When greed barges in wearing a power tie and waving a junk bond, you can transform him into generosity and a passionate desire to contribute to the world. This kind of skill brings a security that nothing can shake.

Listening

FOR DEEPENING YOUR relationships there are few skills so valuable as the ability to listen calmly and attentively to opinions contrary to your own. Normally, we find such listening extremely difficult. Although we consider ourselves adults, deep down most of us still think that every opinion we hold is the ultimate truth. We may appear to be listening, but in our hearts we are thinking, "That's not what I think, so how can it possibly be true?"

In psychological terms, we are identifying ourselves with our opinions – we think that we *are* our opinions. How many marriages are broken because of this? How many friendships? How many countries go to war and sacrifice thousands of innocent lives on this one wrong identification?

Through meditation, which enables you to gain detachment, you can make the marvelous discovery that you are not your opinions. You will be able to listen to opposition with genuine respect and sympathy, yet not get intimidated.

It Takes Two

AS THEY SAY in my mother tongue, "It takes two to get married, and it takes two to quarrel." When you have succeeded in slowing down your thinking process, and making your mind reasonably still, even if somebody quarrels with you, even if they call you names, you will not be a party to the quarrel. As George Bernard Shaw said in his Mephistophelian way, What's the use of hanging a man who doesn't object to hanging?

Sometimes I have heard it called "needling." At certain ages, children especially like to needle their parents. But it is not limited to children. Many people quarrel just to provoke you, to show that you are just as immature as they are. When you oppose them gently but resolutely, they realize that there is no point in needling you. What most of us don't realize is that we let ourselves be needled. If you show that you don't want a needle, or even any thread, that's the end of needling.

I can share an example at my own expense. In a

university, it is not unusual to have severe differences of opinion, which are expressed vividly, since a typical academic has a large fund of words at his or her disposal. While I was teaching at a university in India, I had a colleague who took issue with my opinions on practically every topic. As soon as I saw him coming into the faculty room, I would get up and sit as far away as possible. This only provoked him to make even more upsetting statements and to make sure that I overheard them. By my actions, I was saying, "I am afraid of what you are going to say. I can't withstand your criticism."

Then it dawned on me, "I am now doing well in meditation. Why don't I put it to the test?" I took my courage in both hands and the next time I saw him I went and sat by his side.

He stared at me in disbelief. I don't mind admitting that I was trembling in my shoes. I silently repeated my mantram and then said, "Let me hear those views you were expressing with such candor the other day." He was astonished, but he didn't need a second invitation. This was the chance of a lifetime. Some of my colleagues put down their books and lecture notes and gathered around us, eager to see the battle. My opponent let himself go.

Then the tide turned. I discovered, all of a sudden, that his criticism wasn't affecting my mind at all. All my meditation had paid off. When he came to the end of his lecture, I said thank you and left. He never made those remarks again.

If you really want to test your opinion, take it out and toss it down in front of your opposition. They will jump on it and even dance on it. When they are done, if it is torn, it is not worth keeping.

"I Love Me"

SOMETIMES WHEN I see those huge mobile homes being transported on the freeway, trailing red flags that say WIDE LOAD, I am reminded of certain people I have met and been able to help. Because of the modern emphasis on competition and "looking out for number one," millions of good people have developed such self-will that they seem to need red flags attached to their belts. They block your progress; they make wide turns; they encroach on your lane. When you see them coming, you change lanes to get as far as possible from them.

There is a great example in the scene in *Pride and Prejudice* where Mr. Collins proposes to Elizabeth. When I listen to this extraordinary conversation I hear a most amusing dialogue. Mr. Collins says, "I want you to marry me." Elizabeth asks, "Why?" and Mr. Collins responds, "Because I love me."

If you listen to many conversations between accredited lovers, this is what you will hear. "I want to go to this particular restaurant because I love myself so much." "I insist on seeing this particular play because I am head over heels in love with me." When both people think and act like this, the one emotion that cannot grow is love; the one plant that cannot flourish is the sensitive plant of tenderness.

None of us need be disheartened if we find a fierce level of self-will in ourselves. The very thrust of modern civilization is to inflate self-will in a million little ways. It is simply the conditioning of our times to believe that we will be happy if we can get our way. "Maybe for a little while," say the mystics, "but not for long."

This is not metaphysics but practical psychology. If

your eyes are experienced, you can easily observe, even among a roomful of strangers, who will be easy to live with, who very difficult to live with, and who utterly impossible to live with. Truly loving people express tenderness in innumerable little unconscious ways. They don't need to send cards or write "I love you" across the sky. Just ask yourself, "Am I able to turn my back upon my own pleasure for the sake of the person whom I say I love?" If you are, you are a real lover.

The difficulties between Romeo and Juliet can be minimized if Romeo will put Juliet first, and Juliet will put Romeo first. This is the real secret of romantic relationships. The higher the level of self-will, the greater will be the level of agitation and the lower the level of fulfillment. The lower the level of self-will, the less agitation there will be, and the more loving will be the relationship. And if you ever come across anybody in whom there is no self-will, you will have discovered the greatest lover on earth, with whom it will be a joy to live. With such a person, everything in you will flower in love and beauty.

Loving people are not like mobile homes. They're more like subcompact cars who will gladly give you their lane and say "We'll pull over; you go ahead." Those are the kind of people, according to Jesus, who live in heaven. They get a great deal of joy by putting you first. In the family, if there is one person who does this, his or her example will slowly be assimilated and gradually the home will become harmonious.

Expand Your Capacity to Love

ONE OF THE REASONS we have so many interpersonal problems today is that everyone is constantly being encouraged to concentrate entirely on himself or herself. When you dwell on yourself like this, preoccupied with private profit and personal pleasure, you lose your resilience. A little knock at the door explodes like a pistol shot. A little cracking of knuckles sounds like a machine gun.

On the other hand, when you gradually expand your capacity to love, beginning with your family, but eventually extending to your country, and even the whole world, including the birds of the air and beasts of the field, you will become very secure. If somebody says or does anything against you, you will feel sorry for them. It is not that you will be unaware or that you will connive with them. You will be so secure inwardly that your love will not be affected by anything they say or do. Instead of retaliating, you will be able to give the "soft answer that turneth away wrath."

Such an attitude is beautifully infectious. People – especially children – learn to love through osmosis. Don't think children are as unsophisticated as they are made out to be. When little Johnny is looking at you with those quizzical eyes, or little Emily is snapping her gum, they are seeing right through you. And they are absorbing what they see.

I once heard a story about a mynah bird which developed a very distressing cough. His owner took him to the vet, who listened to the mynah's cough and then said to the owner, "Let me hear you cough." It was the same cough. So the doctor said, "You get over your cough, and the mynah bird will get over your cough too." Similarly, if we want our children to grow up secure and loving, we should turn our backs on profit and pleasure and devote ourselves to putting those around us first.

That is how a home becomes beautiful. I appreciate beauty but, when I visit a home, I am not impressed with expensive furniture and exotic art and elegant gardens. That's not where beauty comes from. It is when I see a family living in harmony, each person putting the other's needs first, that I say to myself, What a beautiful home! This is my idea of the beautiful home – where the father, the mother, and the children always remember the unity of the home, where they turn their backs on their own personal pursuits, on their own personal pleasure and profit, to work together for a higher goal. It is not easy, but it will enable the parents, the children, and even the pets, to flourish.

Family Yoga

They live in wisdom who see themselves in all
and all in them . . .   *– Bhagavad Gita*

AS DIFFICULT AS IT IS to change our
life-style, most of us find it easier to be in harmony with
nature than with all the other people in our lives. It is like
that cartoon I saw where a fellow says "I love the public . . .
it's people I can't stand."

I sometimes call my Eight-Point Program "family
yoga." Nobody need go to a mountain cave to practice
meditation. We can live at our best, pursuing the adventure
of self-discovery through meditation and contributing our
best to the welfare of the world, while living in the midst
of our family and friends and enjoying all the innocent joys
of life.

In fact, as meditation deepens, it is good to extend your
loving relationships to include more and more people. I
live with a very large extended family of friends, which
includes people of many ages, races, and backgrounds, and
I relate to everybody very closely. One of the great joys of
the spiritual life is the opportunity to watch your family
grow to include your neighbors, your whole community,
and eventually the world.

Once Mahatma Gandhi's wife was asked how many
children she had, and she said, "I have only four but my
husband has four hundred million." What that means for
us is that nobody is childless. All the world's children are
our children. Anybody who does anything to harm the
future of the earth is doing harm to their own children.

The ultimate goal of the spiritual life is the realization that while there are five billion people in the world, there is only one Self. This realization opens a perennial fountain of love in your heart. You see yourself in all and everybody in yourself. When any child is hungry, whether in Africa or Asia or in our own country, your love will release a flood of energy and creativity to help alleviate that hunger.

FROM THE EIGHT-POINT PROGRAM:
Spiritual Companionship

THE SANSKRIT WORD for spiritual companionship is satsang, "association with those who are spiritually oriented." When we are trying to change our life, we need the support of others with the same goal.

If you have friends who are meditating along the lines I have suggested, you can get together regularly to share a meal, meditate, and perhaps read an inspirational book aloud. Share your times of entertainment too; relaxation is an important part of spiritual living.

One of the best forms of spiritual association is to work together for a selfless goal like relieving hunger or protecting the environment. Wherever people work like this, without expecting any reward or recognition, their individual capacities are augmented and enhanced. They are unleashing an irresistible force, which, though we may not see it, is going to change our world.

Vaccine for Depression

*Love your enemies, bless them that curse you,
do good to them that hate you, and pray for
them which despitefully use you, and persecute
you; that ye may be the children of your Father
which is in heaven.*
– Jesus, the Sermon on the Mount

AS FAR AS I KNOW, there is no greater
thrill than that of winning over an enemy to be your friend.
That's why Jesus, when he gives us those challenges in the
Sermon on the Mount, says "Bless them that curse you."
Such words are not meant to be declaimed in a pious tone
from the pulpit but to be lived out in the storms and tem-
pests, large and small, which life brings to all of us.

When someone hurts your feelings, or treads heavily on
your pet opinion, that's the test. Jesus would say, "Let's see
your daring! Do good to those that harm you – let us see
your courage!"

I always suggest that you cultivate as many relationships
as possible, working together with other spiritually
inclined people. Then you will have plenty of opportunity
to do things for each other rather than for yourself alone.

That's the kind of opportunity I had as I was growing
up, and therein lies the genius of my teacher, my mother's
mother, who fulfilled herself completely by always forgetting herself in the joy and the welfare of all those around.
That is the only real cure for depression.

It is a prescription that could come from any authentic
spiritual physician. If you dwell upon yourself and your
own private satisfactions, the first disappointment will

throw you into a depression. If you can train yourself to think more and more of the needs of all those around you, to work with people around you even if they are not always pleasant, you will be making yourself immune to depression, and you will be helping others to do the same.

Dharmaputra and His Dog

THERE IS A STORY from the Indian tradition that beautifully illustrates the compassion for all creatures which is the keynote of spiritual ecology. There once lived a king called Dharmaputra, who was the soul of virtue and compassion. When the time came for him to shed his body, he ascended to heaven accompanied by a dog. When he reached heaven's gate, the Indian equivalent of St. Peter looked up his name. "Let's see . . . Dharmaputra. Yes, we have orders to let you in. But we don't have any listing for a dog."

"Won't you please look again?" asked Dharmaputra.

So St. Peter looked up all the rules and said, "I'm sorry, but there is no provision here for dogs."

Dharmaputra did not hesitate. "That dog loves me," he said. "Wherever I go, he goes too, so I have got to take him with me."

St. Peter again considered all the relevant records. "Rules are rules," he said finally. "Either you come in alone, or you go back."

Dharmaputra didn't budge. He said simply, "No dog, no me."

Then a miracle took place. Suddenly, instead of a dog, it was Sri Krishna, the Lord of Love, standing at Dharmaputra's side. St. Peter opened the gates, and, in my version of the story, as Dharmaputra entered heaven Sri Krishna leaned over and whispered, "That was a close shave, wasn't it?"

Little stories like this can remind us to always be compassionate towards our fellow creatures, recognizing that the same Self lives in them as in us. That is the basis for the change I recommend so often – adopting a vegetarian diet. Enjoying a healthy, tasty diet of fresh vegetables, fruits, grains, and nuts is a good way to improve your health, to protect the world's rain forests, and to express your love for all creatures.

For a spiritual ecologist, every creature is sacred. We can do a great deal for the earth by introducing our children to stories like these, and by helping them to cultivate loving relationships with animals and birds. It's very good for them, and it's very good for the creatures too.

A Little Gesture

SELF-WILL OFTEN expresses itself in small but powerful likes and dislikes, which disrupt the harmony of our relationships even if we and the people around us are not entirely aware of it. When we learn to reduce our self-will, and become a little more aware of the needs of others, we can establish harmony in very subtle ways.

I had a clear example of this when I was teaching at my university in India. Throughout my teaching career I have been very fond of the blackboard, getting to the classroom early and filling the board with assignments and recondite Sanskrit and English vocabulary. Unfortunately, the English department in Nagpur used rather small blackboards, so I had my eye on the physics department, which had the biggest blackboards on campus. I contacted the physics faculty, and one of them kindly allowed me to use his lecture hall.

The blackboard was spacious, and I was quite comfortable, except for one thing. Beneath the blackboard was a running groove for the chalk. Every day when I arrived, I found the chalk resting at the far left end of this groove. Since I am right-handed, I moved the chalk to the right end and left it there when I finished.

I didn't think much about it. Every day when I arrived I would say to myself, "Why should this chap always leave the chalk on the left-hand side?" and take it back to the right. Eventually even the students got into the act and enjoyed our confusion.

Then one day it struck me that my physics counterpart must be left-handed. For a few days I left the chalk at the left corner. To my surprise, I began to find the chalk placed carefully at the right corner for me.

Sometimes it takes only a little gesture, a little extra awareness, to bring a restorative harmony into our lives.

Likes and Dislikes

WHEN THE SON of one of my friends was a little boy, he didn't care much for zucchini. That posed a problem since zucchini grew plentifully in our garden and played a principal role in our dinners. So one day when we were talking about soccer, which was his passion, I asked him, "Supposing God appeared before you right now, what would you say?"

"I want to be a soccer star, God."

I said, "Supposing God said, 'If you eat zucchini every day, I will make you the Pelé of California.'"

For a few moments a titanic struggle raged in that young bosom. Finally he said, "I would tell him, 'Thank you, Lord . . . I cannot eat zucchini.'"

Unfortunately, the eating habits of most adults are no more rational. My nutritionist friend Brian tells me that the main problem in nutrition for many people is not that they do not know what is good for their bodies but that, when it comes time to eat, they do not have the will and the discrimination to make the right choices.

I have great sympathy for everyone in that situation and would like to reassure you: our senses can be trained to serve us very faithfully, delighting in what is good for the body and the earth and exercising a healthy caution about more suspect foods. The key to such mastery lies in training the mind to juggle effortlessly with its likes and dislikes. This comes through daily practice.

Training the Senses

IN THE FOOD WE EAT, the books and magazines we read, the movies we see, all of us are subject to the dictatorship of rigid likes and dislikes. To free ourselves from this conditioning, we need to learn to change our likes and dislikes freely when it is in the best interests of those around us or ourselves. We should choose what we eat by what our body needs, for example, rather than by what the taste buds demand.

Similarly, the mind eats, too, through the senses. In this age of mass media, we need to be very discriminating in what we read and what we go to see for entertainment; for we become in part what our senses take in.

Juggling

I KNOW A LITTLE bit about juggling from my own personal experience. When I was in high school I was a bright student and I got tired of hearing my classmates say things like, "All he knows is books," or "Instead of blood he has ink in his veins," and other such things that passed for humor in my high school. I consulted my granny, and she said, "Why don't you learn to juggle?" So I took two lemons and started.

If you have ever tried to juggle, you will know that even with only two lemons it is much harder than it looks. Once the lemons are in motion, it seems like you're juggling not two but twenty-two. But I kept practicing and when I had mastered two, Granny said, "Why don't you add one more?" When I finally unveiled my new skill, my class-mates were astonished.

Similarly, if you are really in love, you will find a great deal of joy in astonishing your partner, your family, or your friends with your ability to juggle effortlessly with your likes and dislikes.

For example, if you happen to take your partner to a res-taurant, you can give the menu to him or her and say, "You order what you like; that's what I will enjoy." You are so much in love that you can enjoy the other person's enjoy-ment. For the most part, this is pretty safe. Usually your partner will order responsibly for you. But once in a while you may end up with a dish that tastes like gall and worm-wood. That will be your finals, the test of true love.

One Thing at a Time

ABOUT TWENTY YEARS AGO my wife and I took a trip to Arizona. As we were driving along one of the beautiful roads there, I looked up to see a sign nailed to the top of a tree. It read, "You should be watching the road." I wanted to answer, "I'm not driving!" but I did appreciate the message.

There is almost a conspiracy in our modern media cul-ture to fragment our attention. We are encouraged to talk on the phone while we drive, to watch television while we eat, to listen to the news while we jog. All these things deplete our capacity to concentrate and reduce our ability to love.

Children in particular suffer from this. When you are listening to a child, try to give your full attention. Those bright little eyes know when your attention is wandering. When the kids are giving you news from school, set your newspaper aside for a moment and listen to every word. You will be training them in how to love.

That's how I was trained by my grandmother, who was my spiritual teacher, and my mother, who was her teaching assistant. When I came back from school every day, Granny would say, "Tell me everything – from the time you left home until the time you came back." I knew that every part of my life was important to her.

So please try to give as much time as possible to your children. Giving them toys or money is not a substitute for this. They will grow up secure and generous, ready to make the world a better place.

One-Pointed Attention

DOING MORE THAN ONE thing at a time
divides attention and fragments consciousness. When we
read and eat at the same time, for example, part of our
mind is on what we are reading and part on what we are
eating; we are not getting the most from either activity.
Similarly, when talking with someone, give him or her
your full attention. These are little things, but all together
they help to unify consciousness and deepen concentration.

Everything we do should be worthy of our full attention.
When the mind is one-pointed it will be secure, free from
tension, and capable of the concentration that is the mark
of genius in any field.

Filling the Inner Needs

VERY EARLY IN MY LIFE my grand-
mother helped me to develop a deep love of nature in a
simple way. She did not rush me here and there for taking
courses and acquiring skills; instead, she gave me lots of
time to understand and admire the beauties of nature.

She considered this the best use of my time and energy.
I have great love for children, and I think we should be
careful not to allow their childhood to be lost. While there
is an important place for lessons and sports, it is not always
doing them a valuable service to rush them from lesson
to lesson.

In my understanding of human development, when our deep, basic needs – for loving attention, for plenty of time to think and understand and grow – are not met while we are still children, we often turn to less desirable means of satisfying them when we grow up.

I always try to give full credit to my grandmother and mother for any success that has come my way. They filled all my deepest needs by the time I left high school. Today, with no childhood needs that have to be met, I can enjoy life in full freedom. I have no special need for money or pleasure or profit or prestige: through the love of these two women I came to understand that these things won't add anything to me. Inwardly full, I have only one need: to give.

When children grow up with this kind of inner fullness, they have no need to exploit the environment. They can enjoy all the innocent joys of life while using their talents, time, and resources to protect the earth. According to an ancient Sanskrit saying, any parent who has raised such a child – a young man or woman who lives to give – has fulfilled their highest purpose in life.

Eating in Peace

WHEN I FIRST CAME to this country, one of the things that used to surprise me was to see people walking and eating at the same time. There was a café in Berkeley in those days called "Eat and Run." Students patronized it in large numbers, so I used to tell my class, "Why not have another café, 'Drink and Jump'?"

You won't find me eating at "Eat and Run." Trying to do many things at once means doing nothing well. As the Buddha says, "When you are walking, walk. When you are sitting, sit. Don't wobble." I would add, "When you are eating, eat. When you are running, run."

From my experience I have found that it adds immeasurably to the joy of a meal not to rush through it alone or "on the go," but to share it with others in a relaxed manner. This is one of the great secrets of a simple, beautiful life: nourishment comes not only from what you eat, but from how you eat it and from the company with whom you eat.

In the Bible there is a beautiful prayer: "Give us this day our daily bread." "Bread" here means much more than what we use to make sandwiches. In the Hindu tradition as much as in the Christian, meals are not secular activities. They are considered sacraments, because they fill our deeper needs, not only physically, but emotionally, mentally, and spiritually. Eating is much more than four food groups and the principal amino acids. To live and give at our best, we need to eat in peace, in an atmosphere of love.

Whosoever Saves Time
Shall Lose It

ACCORDING TO A REPORT I read
recently, depression affects fifteen million Americans. If
you include their families, that figure grows to about fifty
million people. If the Buddha were here to comment, he
would have a very precise diagnosis: many of these depres-
sions arise because we simply don't have time for one of
the richest fulfillments life has to offer – loving personal
relationships.

There is a paradox hidden at the root of our fast-paced
life-style: the more time we try to save by hurrying, the less
time we seem to have. In South India where I grew up,
nobody tried to save time, yet we always had lots of it.
One might almost say in the manner of Jesus, "Whosoever saves time shall lose it."

Everywhere today – on the freeways, in the stores, in
our schools – the motto is faster, faster, faster, faster. We try
to squeeze so much into our day that we end up with
little time for anything, least of all relationships. Being a
good mother or father, brother or sister, friend or colleague,
requires a lot of patience, and patience takes time.

One simple way to start deepening your relationships
is to make it a point to listen carefully to your children or
partner or neighbor every day. I do this myself. I listen with
complete concentration to our children over meals, to their
accounts of school, to what they will be doing on the weekend. This can take some patience, since children often give

detailed and even fanciful accounts of their activities, but every minute you spend this way helps build an atmosphere of love which will protect them and you from the inevitable ups and downs of life.

Finding Time

AS A MEDITATION teacher, I frequently hear people say, "I don't have time to do everything that I have to do already – and you're asking me not just to slow down but to set aside a half hour for meditation? Impossible!"

I have a lot of sympathy, because I too was in that position. When I took to meditation I was teaching on a very active campus, with many interests and many friends, and with many meetings to attend. I wanted to simplify my life immediately but didn't know how. As an experiment, I made a long catalog of all my duties, responsibilities, recreation, and entertainment. I looked at it and said to myself, "No wonder there is no time for meditation or even reading spiritual books!"

Then I went through with a red pencil, striking off every item that was neither necessary nor beneficial. It didn't break my heart, but I did feel a few twinges of regret. How could I bring myself not to attend these meetings, not to go to those concerts? But I persisted and, when I was through, I had found a lot of time.

But here's the awful part: I thought people would miss

me at the meetings, but they didn't. No one even said, "Where were you?" That was the unkindest cut of all.

So go through your list and use the red pencil firmly. Past conditioning can make it rather painful, but you will be gaining precious time for enriching your life and healing the earth.

Tender and Tough

WHEN I TALK ABOUT putting others first I don't mean you need always to say, "Honey, you ask, I do," or "Right-o, sweetie; you command, I carry out." Not at all. Real love is a harmonious combination of both tenderness and toughness.

That's what romance is really about. If you are about to do something unwise, threatening to harm yourself or those around you, a truly loving person will stand in your way with tender arms outstretched, always respecting you but never conniving with your weakness. That kind of opposition is an art we must learn if we are to establish harmony, not just with our family and friends, but in our work, in our community, in the world.

It requires a lot of security and toughness inside, because in the early days the person may return your letters and sonnets, and say, "Even if I never see you again, it will be too soon." That is when romance blossoms. You stand firmly rooted in love and you say, "You may not care for me, but I care for you. You may not love me, but I love you. You may run away from me, but my love will follow you to the ends of the earth." This is romantic love that not even Cleopatra and Antony could rival. Instead of bringing about each other's ruin, this love brings fulfillment. When your partner's mind becomes calm he or she will say, "Here is somebody who cares, somebody who really loves me."

No Longer Ruled by Fear

THROUGH YEARS and years of difficult, sometimes monotonous practice, I have acquired a skill which more than repays the effort I spent. Now, on those occasions when somebody is discourteous to me, which is rare, I find it natural to be more courteous; when somebody is unkind, to be more kind; when somebody is moving away from me, to be more supportive.

This is how you establish harmony. There is nobody who does not respond slowly, gradually, to this kind of love that tires out its opposition, a love that will not let you go. When we encourage young people to develop such love – by doing it ourselves – they respond beautifully. It is the kind of challenge that draws out their highest capacities.

Nevertheless, it does go against the grain of our human conditioning. We are conditioned to be always on guard, in case a certain somebody, a kind of thorn-in-the-flesh, might be coming around the next corner. If we see him we want to be ready to make our escape, duck out through the next door into a dark alley and disappear into the night.

Instead, when you have acquired this extraordinary

skill, you are no longer ruled by fear. If you see Mr. Thorn approaching, you may actually decide to go and meet him. "He's going to be unpleasant," you say to yourself. "What an opportunity!" "She's going to be discourteous; I can help her by being courteous and calm."

When I used to present this in the early sixties, the beatniks of San Francisco, whom I liked very much, used to say, "Man, that's all topsy-turvy!"

"No," I used to say, "everything is topsy-turvy now. When you can act like this, then the world will be righted."

Learning to Hiss

Be ye therefore wise as serpents, and harmless as doves. — Jesus, Matthew 10:16

MY TEACHER, my grandmother, made me aware very early in life that gentleness is the mark of real strength and courage. When I see a person bursting out in anger, or trying to retaliate for some offense, I always remember her laconic words: "Weak people . . . no stamina at all."

It takes real fortitude to be gentle even under attack. But don't think that such gentleness is passive in any sense of the word. Being gentle doesn't mean that you don't express your opposition when people are doing something which hurts themselves or others or the earth. When you feel deeply the unity of life, you will also feel the need to express your opposition to anything which violates that unity.

To be gentle in our rough world is a demanding art, but it is one we all can master. Many of the great mystics lived as we do in the midst of society, and they learned to function freely even when people were unappreciative and hostile. From their own practical experience these mystics say that you need to pretend to a certain amount of aloofness when dealing with people who want to harm you. Inwardly, you always remain full of love, even for your enemies, but outwardly you pretend that you will not allow your kindness to be taken advantage of. It's a kind of play that you act out.

To illustrate, there is a little story told by the great Indian mystic, Sri Ramakrishna. One day a spiritual teacher was passing through a village and saw some children who were chasing a snake. They were tormenting it with sticks and stones. The teacher could understand the pain of the snake. He sent the children away and he shared his spiritual wisdom with the snake. "These children are hurting you because you try to harm them. Don't try to bite these kids. That is why they are hurting you." And the spiritual teacher went on his way.

After a few weeks the teacher returned to find the snake had become so thin, it was about to die. "What happened?" asked the teacher. The snake said, "You told me never to bite the kids, and they have been tormenting me. I've just been hiding in my hole."

The teacher said, "Oh no! I told you not to bite them, but I didn't tell you not to hiss."

The Marriage of True Minds

ONCE WHEN I WAS teaching at the
University of California at Berkeley, one of my students
tried to put me on the spot. "I have the choice of marrying
for money or for sex," he said. "What would you advise?"

He was sure that he had placed me on the horns of a
dilemma, but I thrive on such dilemmas. The audience
lifted the roof when I answered, "If that is the only choice
you have – sex or money – I recommend strongly that you
marry for money. It will last a little longer."

I am all in favor of romantic relationships, but I would
like to caution everyone – not only young people but also
older people who are being caught in this trap – that
romance is not based on sex. That is a superstition encouraged by television and popular magazines to sell everything from shaving cream to shampoo to shoes. Real
romance is based on increasing tenderness and increasing
respect for each other. Without such tenderness and
respect, a relationship cannot last. In the end it will bring
only suffering.

There is a beautiful place for sex in a completely loyal,
completely loving relationship, but it needs to be pointed
out that the nature of a purely physical relationship is to
pall and become stale, to lose its freshness and appeal.
When such relationships fail it doesn't reflect on anybody's
capacity to love. That is simply the nature of a physical
relationship.

Atomic physics provides an interesting perspective here.
A physicist will tell you that your body and the body of
your sweetheart are not solid. They appear solid only

because of our imprecise instruments of observation. However painful it may be for us to hear it, our bodies are mostly space, and the little bit which is not space is changing every moment, getting older, losing its resilience, strength, and energy. This is a hard blow at physical romance. How can you be permanently in love with something that is mostly space? So don't blame yourself or anybody else if a physical relationship doesn't last. There was very little there in the first place.

On the other hand, there is no more dependable and delightful basis for a romantic relationship than two people working together for a great cause that is bigger than themselves, forgetting their personal differences in making the world a little greener for all. In Shakespeare's lovely phrase, this is a "marriage of true minds," which only grows more beautiful with the passage of time.

Romance

LAST FEBRUARY fourteenth, I took a walk through the local mall to see how people were celebrating St. Valentine's Day, the holiday dedicated to romance. In one shop there were huge heart-shaped cookies, embossed with messages in frosting. (The cookies, I hope, were fresher than the clichés.) In another shop window there was a selection of chocolate hearts with a sign saying "All you need for one of these hearts is love and thirteen dollars." I couldn't help wondering, What does all this have to do with romance?

While I was growing up in India, our nation was lifted up by a love which soared high above what we often refer to as romance. For over fifty years, Mahatma Gandhi and his wife, Kasturbai Gandhi, set us a rare example of love which, in Shakespeare's phrase, "bears it out even to the edge of doom." When everything is wrong, when everything is against you, that's when such love blossoms into splendor. Only someone like Shakespeare, a great exponent of the highest love, could have written those words, and it took the faith and courage of the Gandhis to live it.

At times, the edge of doom must have seemed very close to the Gandhis, yet their love only grew with every trial. Threatened by the government, thrown into prison, attacked by extremists, their property confiscated, their relatives banished – this was the climate in which their love blossomed and inspired four hundred million of us to give our all to the cause of nonviolence and freedom.

A Bridge

*What wisdom can you find that is greater than
kindness?*   – *Jean Jacques Rousseau*

THROUGH CONSTANT practice it is
possible to make your life a permanent gift to your family
and the world. You can become a kind of Christmas tree
all year long. Any time your children or your partner or
your parents are in pain or discomfort, when they are afraid
or uneasy, they can come and help themselves to your love
and security.

It is not possible to achieve such inner peace without
becoming deeply aware of the needs of those around you.
Highly self-willed people always find it difficult to love
because, while they may have a bright intellect and a great
deal of wealth, they react immediately to the least provocation. If you are angry, they will retaliate. If you are afraid,
they will be insecure. That's just human conditioning,
which I sometimes call the jukebox response: you put in
your quarter and the old, familiar tune comes out.

Some psychologists have claimed that stimulus and
response is the basis of all human behavior. I disagree.
There are some glorious exceptions – the great spiritual
teachers of all the major religions, who have shown that if
you want to love more and more, it is possible to cut the
nexus between what others do to you and what you do to
them.

According to these spiritual figures, in order to call
yourself a lover, you must be free from the need to react;
you must be free to respond as you consider best. If

somebody is unkind to you, you can choose to be kind to that person, which is the best way to win him over. If somebody slanders you, you can choose not to be intimidated or upset, but to bide your time and try to help her when she is calmer. That is what deep love can do.

You can see how much the world needs such people. Wherever they live, they will be a bridge between individuals, between races, even between nations. According to the English mystic William Law, such "love has no errors, for all errors are the want of love."

PART THREE

Finding Harmony with
the Earth

Waking Up

IT IS SAID that when the Compassionate Buddha entered a town, he radiated such security and joy that crowds gathered around him just to gaze at his face.

"Blessed One," they asked timidly, "are you a god?"

"No," he said.

"Are you an angel?"

"No."

"Are you a prophet?"

"No."

"Then what are you?"

"I am awake."

This is the literal, etymological meaning of the word Buddha, from the Sanskrit root *budh,* "to wake up."

When I was teaching at a university in India, I believed I was fully conscious, fully awake. I was quite certain that all my colleagues were awake and that even my students were awake. I was fully active in what we normally call waking life: pursuing private satisfactions, making money, accumulating material possessions, trying to get recognition. Such a life, the Buddha would say with compassion, is the life of a somnambulist. I was sleep-walking, sleep-teaching, sleep-living.

Today, if we look around, we can see that we live in a sleeping society – asleep and dreaming of wealth and pleasure and power even as the environmental foundations of our lives are being eroded by the unconscious forces of greed, ignorance, and hostility.

It is only when you wake up that you begin to see that there is a whole other world inside of you, as real as the world without. In that inner world lies the key to establishing harmony with the environment and healing the world around us.

From Wasteful to Simple

HENRY DAVID THOREAU raised a provocative question: "What is the use of a house if you haven't got a tolerable planet to put it on?" It's hard to answer. What is the use of science and art and dancing and music if our way of life is making the earth uninhabitable?

I love music and the fine arts; I have always been a fan of classical dance and theater; I have deep respect for the beneficial accomplishments of science. But all of these take second place in my heart behind the art of living in harmony with the earth, with others, and with myself – not because I don't love the arts and sciences but because, as Thoreau would say, if you don't have a good planet to put it on, what's the use of having the best western home in California? Among all our activities our first priority should be to change our mode of living from wasteful to simple, from thoughtless to elegant, from destructive to sustainable.

It is not always glamorous work to slowly change your habits and help others to change theirs, to dismantle the old and quietly build a new life. Probably no one will give you a Nobel Prize or an Oscar for having worked to protect the earth, but deep inside you will feel the joy of having contributed. You will have won the respect of the hardest person to please in the world: yourself.

Seeing the Unity of Life

BEFORE I TOOK TO meditation, I had read many times about the unity underlying the seeming diversity of life, both in Western and Eastern writers, but until I had travelled deep into my consciousness through meditation, I could not have believed that the world really is one, that all of us are one. The sun, the moon, the stars, the ocean, the rivers, the forests, we are all one family. That is the lesson our environmental crisis is trying to teach us.

Learning to see the unity of life is a little like breaking a secret code. When I was a boy scout in India, like boy scouts everywhere I had to learn Morse code. On a special occasion when the local school inspector came, my cousin and I were chosen to demonstrate our communications skills. The inspector gave me a message which I transmitted with flags to my cousin, who was standing fifty yards away. Dot dash dot, dot dot dash, and so forth. If an onlooker didn't know the code, he would have wondered why these fellows were waving their flags. But anyone who knew the code would be able to follow.

William Blake, who broke through life's code, said that when he looked at the rising sun he saw not just a glowing disk of fire somewhat like a guinea, but a host of angels singing, "Holy, Holy, Holy." If you tell William Blake that you don't hear the angels, he will say, "You have earplugs in your ears; how do you expect to hear? Pull them out and then you will hear."

Meditation enables us to interpret the code of all life. We learn to remove the earplugs and blindfold which keep us from knowing the unity. Gradually, we gain a new mode of perception. When we look at a forest, for example, we begin to understand that botany is not the only way to study trees. Just as there is a biological aspect to trees, there is a spiritual aspect from which we can learn: it is a tree's nature to give. You and I give gifts on Christmas – only to people whom we like, and only when they have gifts for us. For a tree, however, it is Christmas every day and night. A fir tree doesn't say, "Here is oxygen only for people I like." A mango tree doesn't say, "I won't give you mangoes because you don't like me." They say to everybody, "Come help yourselves. What we give is free for all."

Gradually, we can learn to give something back to these trees to show them our love. That doesn't mean writing sonnets and hanging them on their trunks. To show love for trees means simply to speak their language: plant them, look after them, fertilize them, prune them, protect them, and let them grow to their full height. They will express their love by giving us oxygen and feeding us.

An Expression of Love

Trees bend low with ripened fruit;
Clouds hang down with gentle rain;
Noble men bow graciously.
This is the way of generous things.
                                      – Bhartrihari

BETWEEN THE SURFACE of the earth and outer space we have only about forty miles of atmosphere. Imagine – for five billion people, we have only forty miles of air. Without the constant renewal which trees and other plants provide, we would eventually exhaust our oxygen. The only reason we are here and our children's children will be here is that trees and plants are renewing our oxygen supply.

While I lived in India I had some European friends who poked fun at the Indian custom of worshiping trees. "You people worship banyan trees, don't you?" they would say. I enjoyed replying with humor but also with truth, "No, I worship *every* tree!" Trees give us the air and food we need to live. That's the way God expresses his love. He doesn't come directly and say, "Here, open this envelope. There are some coupons inside. You can go and buy love wherever it is available." As some of the simplest and greatest mystics say, God's love is taking place in front of our eyes. The trees say, "Give me your carbon dioxide; I'll give you oxygen in return." What greater act of love can there be?

Seeing Love in the Sun

IN THE BHAGAVAD GITA the Lord says,
"Among luminaries I am the sun." This is to remind us that
we depend for our very life on the sun and the many physical and biological forces which filter and harness the sun's
rays. In the traditional language of religion, this complex
network of forces is beautiful proof of the Lord's love for
us.

Without the sun, we would have no food. Everything
we eat contains a generous helping of sunlight. The leaves
of the plants and trees are solar collectors trained to catch
the sun's energy and turn it into gourmet cuisine. The mystics ask, "Who but a lover would do all this?" Just as on St.
Valentine's Day you present your sweetheart with flowers,
the Self, which lives in every one of those plants and trees,
is giving us the very best food every day.

In the Western tradition, St. Francis of Assisi gives
beautiful expression to our kinship with the sun when he
addresses it as Brother Sun. He is reminding us that all of
us – even the stars and planets – belong to the same family.
When we get carried away with personal profit and forget
that we belong to this family, the results are always
disastrous.

Whether you call it God's love, or Nature's providence,
or lucky coincidence, the earth's stratospheric ozone layer
is perfectly balanced to protect us against the sun's ultraviolet rays. Now, however, that protective shield is being
severely damaged by industrial chemicals produced and
used primarily to make a profit. The increase in harmful

ultraviolet rays may lead not only to increased incidence of skin cancer but to disruptions in our food chain as well.

Although we first learned in 1974 that chlorofluorocarbons deplete the ozone layer, after twenty years we still have not completely eliminated CFCs. Urged on by an exaggerated desire for profit, we have unwittingly disrupted the delicate network of forces which protect our health and future. Let us make sure this never happens again. There is a place for profit in every business, but our first concern should always be to keep our business and our lives in harmony with the forces which preserve life.

At Home in the Universe

Covet nothing. All belongs to the Lord. Thus working may you live a hundred years. Thus alone will you work in real freedom.
                                    – Isha Upanishad

IN SPIRITUAL TERMS, the very taproot of the environmental movement is that everything belongs to the one Self who lives in the hearts of all people and creatures, and even insects and plants.

In practical terms that means nothing on earth is ours to destroy. Nobody has any right to pollute the air, water, or seas, to cut down forests, or to wash away the topsoil. We do not own the earth. We are just transients who have been entrusted to leave the earth a little better than we found it.

This is everybody's job; nobody is exempt from it and, in this sense, nobody is unemployed.

It follows that our environmental crisis demands that every one of us play a useful part, in our own way, to improve the environment wherever we live. If a person fails to do that, even if he makes a lot of money or if she wins a prestigious prize, the Buddha would say, "You haven't done what you have to do."

When you have done what you have to do, you will feel very secure, very fulfilled. As you discover the Self in your own heart, you discover it simultaneously everywhere, in the people and creatures around you. You will feel very much at home in this universe. You don't need to take my word for it. Try it and see for yourself.

Your Essence Is Kindness

Ahimsa (nonviolence) is for Gandhi the basic law of our being. That is why it can be used as the most effective principle for social action, since it is in deep accord with the truth of man's nature, and corresponds to his innate desire for peace, justice, order, freedom, and personal dignity .
— Thomas Merton

WHEN I WAS TEACHING freshmen in my junior college in India, I noticed that they had a curious difficulty: they would confuse the English words "invent" and "discover." As I graded their papers, I often ran across sentences like, "The telescope was discovered by Galileo." I hit upon a simple means of showing them the difference between inventing and discovering.

I would take a piece of chalk in one hand, cover it, and say, "I have covered it. Now I open my hand, and you have discovered it." Afterwards they never said Galileo discovered telescopes.

The same is true for the abiding love – what Gandhi called ahimsa – that dwells in the depths of our hearts. You don't have to invent it, or buy it, or borrow it, or steal it from a saint. You have already got it. It is in you, but it is covered so thickly that you don't suspect that your very nature is love, your very essence is kindness. This is the discovery that you make when you bring your mind to stillness through the practice of meditation and the allied disciplines. Afterwards, you can function beautifully in all aspects of your life, living with your family, working at a clinic or a campus or a store, and be a living influence for kindness, goodness, and love, wherever you choose to play your part.

Ahimsa

Nonviolence is the supreme law of life.
— Hindu Proverb

ONE OF THE GREATEST sayings to come
down the ages in India is *ahimsa paramo dharma. Parama*
means "supreme." *Dharma* means "law, support, fulfillment." *Himsa* means "injury," so *ahimsa* means "non-
injury." It sounds negative in English, but what the saying
implies is that when all desire to injure others or the environment has subsided, we shall find ourselves in our native
state, loving and respecting all – not only the world of
people, but also the world of nature.

This supreme law has been violated by the whole
world, not only in our relations with other nations and
other races but also in the way we treat the earth.

Behind this little word "ahimsa" is the revolutionary
implication that if you can remove from your consciousness this age-old, race-old tendency to hurt others through
words, deeds, and thoughts, you will see God, the Self, in
your own heart.

So although ahimsa seems like a series of *don'ts,* it
leads to a series of *dos.* If you don't encourage resentment,
hostility, self-will, or selfishness in your mind, your mind
will naturally fill in the *dos,* growing more secure, more
loving, and more effective in its work.

A Life of Peace

> *I have known from early youth that nonviolence is not a cloistered virtue to be practiced by the individual for his peace and final salvation, but it is a rule of conduct for the whole of society.*
> – *Mahatma Gandhi*

USUALLY, THE CONCEPT of nonviolence is applied only to violence between human beings or nations, but having thought it over and experimented with it for many years, I have learned from Gandhi to apply it to almost all aspects of daily living.

The primary cause of the environmental crisis is our society's attitude that nature is ours to dominate and exploit for our own benefit. This is a great violence we do to the earth, a violence which needs to be opposed – gently but firmly – with the nonviolence of a simple, sustainable life, lived in love and respect for all.

So what Gandhiji stands for when he places the ideal of ahimsa before us is not patchwork reform in politics or economics, changing a little here or there. Rather, he says, we must go deep within ourselves and change the very basis of our attitude towards the environment, towards others, towards ourselves.

"They Ain't Makin' Real Estate No More"

THROUGH DEFORESTATION and modern industrial agricultural methods – the methods of "agribusiness" – the world is losing twenty-four billion tons of topsoil every year. The United States is no exception. Iowa once had an average of sixteen inches of topsoil. Now it has been reduced to one half, just eight inches. We call this progress. Every year we peel off another layer of skin from our Mother Earth. How long can it last? As an American humorist said, "They ain't makin' real estate no more."

I look back with great respect to the days of my boyhood in South India, when we were trained never to do anything to deprive our living Mother Earth of her skin. For us, agriculture was taught not only in schools and colleges. It was a way of life passed down from generation to generation, and every new generation had the opportunity to improve a little upon it. I have coined a phrase for this way of life: *agridharma,* from *agri,* meaning "field," and *dharma,* meaning "law or divine order." It is an entire way of life, which respects the needs of the earth and all creatures even as it seeks to fill the needs of human beings.

When you raise your own vegetables and fruits, when you buy locally grown organic produce, when you adopt a vegetarian diet to help protect the rain forests, you are helping to replace agribusiness with agridharma, violence with love.

Possessed by Love

Let me be possessed by love . . .
– Thomas a Kempis

MYSTICS FROM ALL the world's traditions
are fond of warning us never to be possessed by things. If
you look carefully at any paper or magazine you will see
that, while our modern civilization has contributed a great
deal towards making our life more comfortable, it has also
been conditioning us slowly but surely not to possess
things, but to be possessed by them. The conditioning can
be easily observed. The proof is that when we think we
cannot have something we want, whether it is a new dress
or a new car, we feel inadequate, incomplete.

This strange inadequacy, which the media exploits, is
the source of a popular modern phenomenon, impulse buying. You go to a shopping center to have a cup of cocoa,
and you come back with a big brown bag full of things. If I
ask you why, you answer, "They were on sale." I have
never been able to understand the logic of this. If you don't
need something, what does it matter whether it is on sale or
whether you can have two for one or eight for seven? Such
"bargains" appeal to that hidden feeling of inadequacy.

But we can free ourselves. As the mystics say, when you
learn to still your mind through meditation you will begin
to see the light of the Self – who lives not outside you but
in the depths of your heart – shining on the mountains, the
sea, the forests, and all living creatures. Once this experience comes to you, you will be free to love. Even when you
need to buy things, you will remember not to be possessed
by them, but to possess them in freedom.

A Garbage Experiment

I WAS AMAZED to read that every man, woman, and child in our country generates twice his or her weight in waste every day. This garbage habit affects not only our own country. Our growing refuse pile now spills over our borders through what is called "garbage imperialism." As our landfills fill up, we are sending our waste, much of it toxic, to poor Third World countries desperate for the meager income it brings.

So I suggest that all of us perform a little experiment. Keep a waste journal. It's a very good project for children, and an even better project for adults, to observe and calculate how this mountain of waste is generated. Then gradually cut down your waste from two times your weight to one. You see, I am not a revolutionary but an evolutionary. Generate only enough waste to equal your weight. If you are more ambitious, you can reduce your weight.

This has nothing to do with capitalism or socialism or any other -ism; this has everything to do with love of children. Every child everywhere is entitled to the reasonable comforts of life. No child's country should be treated as a dump. I follow my grandmother's way of changing my habits: not being forced by laws or public opinion or peer pressure, but impelled by love.

Contentment

THE BUDDHA GIVES A compassionate explanation for the impulse which keeps us buying and throwing away more and more things. He calls it *tanha,* which means "thirst" – a thirst that parches our souls. Madison Avenue encourages us to slake that thirst by drinking salt water.

Remember the words of Jesus to the woman at the well? When he was thirsty, the woman gave him cool water to drink. Jesus, by way of thanking her, says, "Whosoever drinketh of this water shall thirst again. But whosoever drinketh of the water that I shall give him shall never thirst." Once you become aware of the Self, your thirst is quenched. You no longer need anything from the world.

When I was walking with my wife around a big shopping center a few days ago, I told her that even if they offered me everything free, I really wouldn't want anything. That doesn't mean I don't like to buy things that are useful, comfortable, and necessary, or to make the best of my personal appearance, but I have no craving for those things. Through many years of meditation, I now find my contentment within, and my thirst has been quenched. Instead of having a sense of inadequacy or incompleteness when faced with such a bewildering array of items, I feel a great joy wherever I look: How many beautiful jackets I don't need! How many pairs of shoes I don't even have to look at! I'm a free man. I can make original choices unpressured by the mass media.

I am not wealthy, but because of this precious skill, which anyone can learn, I know how it is to be a millionaire. Once I asked a millionaire friend of mine, "Tell me, what does it mean to be a millionaire?"

"Ah," she said, "I can tell you that there is this feeling of freedom, wherever I go." That's the kind of freedom I have, but it is not dependent on stocks or shares. It comes from within. My greatest desire is that everyone may discover the tremendous wealth that all of us possess within, simply by virtue of being a human being.

"Heart Roots" Revolution

WHILE I ADMIRE some of the great strides modern civilization has made, particularly during this century, I must point out that our progress has involved a great deal of violence towards nature. When someone asks me to appraise the twentieth century, I always place its conveniences and technical advances on one side of the balance and put the injury to nature on the other.

The prevailing opinion seems to be that technology is an end in itself. We use technology now on the slightest provocation, whether the situation truly warrants it or not: in medicine, education, cooking, entertainment, and sports. By contrast, I take every opportunity to remind people that technology is only a means. It can never be an end. Isn't it Barry Commoner who reminds us that the danger of technology is not in its failure but its success?

I am all for "high tech" when it is combined with high ideals, but it is up to people like you and me to say, very politely but persuasively, "If there is any suspicion that this product is detrimental to the environment, we won't buy it and we will ask our friends not to buy it." That is my way – no demonstrations or violence against anybody – just an appeal to people's good sense through love and education. That is the way a revolution can spread: not just growing from grass roots but from "heart roots" as well.

Getting Out of the Fast Lane

I FIRST CAME TO the United States over thirty years ago on an ocean liner. When I got out at New York after a leisurely month-long journey, I couldn't believe what I saw on the streets around me. I thought I had arrived just in time for an automobile race.

As fast as the pace of life then seemed to me, I have seen its speed increase dramatically during the past thirty years. Today we seem to be always in a hurry. Just to save a few minutes, we take a car when we could walk or ride the bus; we eat overprocessed, "microwavable" food on the run, and throw away millions of tons of the plastic, paper, and polystyrene foam it is packaged in, along with the countless disposable plastic utensils with which we eat it.

And yet, what do we do with all those minutes we save? I wish we could say that we use them to deepen our relationships, or to come to a fuller understanding of who we are and why we are here. But all too often, driven by the sheer momentum of modern life, we waste that time in pursuits which do little to improve life for ourselves or others. The earth suffers from this, of course, but so do we. In the internal environment of our hearts, we are neglecting and even damaging our most precious source of fulfillment: the capacity to love.

Slow, Simple, Beautiful, Loving

THERE IS A CLOSE connection between slowing down, living simply, and bringing beauty and love into our lives.

The economist E. F. Schumacher made a deep impression on millions of people with his book *Small Is Beautiful,* and I have often thought of writing a companion volume called *Slow Is Beautiful.* As George Bernard Shaw used to ask, how is the person traveling three hundred miles per hour more civilized than the person traveling three miles per hour?

I am not a champion of poverty – no one anywhere should have to live in poverty – but I am a champion of simplicity. To me, the simple life is beautiful, artistic, and esthetically satisfying. It produces the maximum effect with a minimum of means. Far too often our modern technology, despite its ingenuity, produces just the opposite: the minimum effect with the maximum of means. According to a saying in my mother tongue, Malayalam, we are using a sword to cut a ribbon.

This is not an issue for governments or corporations to solve. If every man and woman will try to simplify life in accordance with their needs and the context in which they live, they will find they have plenty of time to love.

Although "love" has become a common word today, it is frequently used without any understanding of what an uncommon thing it really is. People talk about falling in love like falling into a manhole. It's not at all that easy. We need time, a slow pace, and a simple life to gain some understanding of what love is.

Two in a Car

BY NOW ALL OF US have heard the scientists' warnings that our industrial society – which I am sometimes tempted to call our "chemical civilization" – releases so much carbon dioxide and other heat-trapping gases that our planet may become a kind of hothouse during the next century, with disastrous effects for all of life – if, that is, all of us don't join together to prevent it.

Governments and big business have an important role to play, but there is no need to wait for them. The answer is as close as the nearest freeway. Next time you go out for a ride, look around at the other cars. The vast majority carry only one person. To reduce your personal automotive emissions by fifty percent, all you need to do is follow a simple and elegant suggestion: don't drive alone – travel with at least two in a car.

That's where slowing down comes in. Carpooling often means that you have to go to your friend's home and wait a while – talk to the children, play with the dog, or sit in your car and repeat your mantram. Everybody can do this. Perhaps it means starting a little earlier or going a little out of your way, but that is the art of living in wisdom. Waiting a few minutes for a friend gradually becomes a joy. You start thinking differently, not just about yourself and your time, but about your friends, the air, and the earth.

Of course there are some occasions when you will have to travel alone, but you can always be on the lookout for people to share your ride, your tires, your car, your company. I am a great idealist. If only we could persuade people to travel four in a car, just imagine what a different scene there would be on the freeways! Day by day, little people like you and me can bring about a quiet, unobtrusive revolution.

Allah's Bounty

I HAVE HEARD that King Faisal, one of the founders of Saudi Arabia, didn't keep flowers or photographs on his desk. Instead, he displayed a flask of petroleum and a card saying, "Allah's bounty." It is a good reminder to all of us. Even petroleum belongs not to any country or multinational company but to the one Self who lives in all of us and in our children. It is ours only as a trust, to use wisely, with a keen awareness of the needs of the future.

I couldn't get over it when I read that we are well on our way to exhausting the earth's fossil fuels – coal, oil, natural gas – which have taken millions and millions of years to accumulate. And we have done it in only a hundred years, polluting the air and disrupting the chemical balance of the atmosphere. I would like to say to petroleum magnates and to any driver who has forgotten to consider the future: "What about your children, and your children's children, and their children's children – don't you think they would appreciate breathing fresh air?"

I do not say that you must never drive alone, but anyone who does not try to carpool and cut back on driving alone is not fulfilling the terms of the trust. It comes with being a human being. Although I am glad that the authorities are encouraging car pools, I find it embarrassing when I take three people across the Golden Gate and the man says that we don't have to pay. I almost feel like saying, "I am grateful, but you don't have to bribe me. I'm doing this for my own good and for the good of all."

Speed

I ONCE HEARD ABOUT a funeral for the automobile to be held, appropriately enough, in Berkeley, California. Although I appreciated the humor, I did not go, because that is not my way. I am not at all against the judicious use of the automobile. But when it threatens the lives of young people, I cannot patiently put up with it.

In recent years the speed of life has grown so insidiously – almost without our being aware of it – that we are not alarmed that nearly fifty thousand people, many of them teenagers, meet with death on American roads every year, and an additional two million are injured, some of them paralyzed for life. It is the price we pay for speed, and we shouldn't put up with it. We need to ask ourselves, What is the use of all this speed? What do we gain by it?

When you exceed the fifty-five-miles-per-hour speed limit, you are playing russian roulette with your life and with the earth's climate. That is why I support a reasonable speed limit, which saves lives, petroleum, and the atmosphere.

Keeping to the speed limit is one way to show love for our children. And we can write to our legislators and the mass media to say, "No, we don't want to increase the speed. Far too many young people lose their lives on the highways every year." That is the mark of love. When your heart is full of love for young people, you will find it easy to say, "We don't mind reaching San Francisco five minutes later."

The Two-Thirds World

AS YOU MAKE these beneficial changes in your life, it is good to remember that they will play a part in enriching the quality of life not just for you and your family, but perhaps, through the power of example, for your country and even the whole world.

It is only when you go into Third World countries and live there for a long time that you can grasp the enormous influence the affluent West exerts, particularly the United States of America. Even those who have briefly visited such countries cannot imagine how much Third World societies admire and emulate the Americans they meet or see on television.

For that reason, we have a great responsibility to encourage these countries through our personal example to live and develop their industries in a sustainable manner, using the best of appropriate technology while at the same time maintaining their respect for the environment and the traditional wisdom of their ancestors. It is my deep desire that with our help they will be able to avoid some of the harmful mistakes that we have made.

According to experts in world resources, the welfare of these developing countries cannot be separated from our own. As one bright journalist puts it, the Third World should really be called the Two-Thirds World, since it contains at least that many of the world's men, women, and children.

If this Two-Thirds World follows our path of intense production, consumption, and waste, it will prove a disaster not only for them but for us. Per capita, the United States uses seventy times more paper and paperboard – much of it packaging – than many Third World countries. If they were to follow our lead, how long would our forests last?

We need the Third World's cooperation to protect the forests that balance the earth's climate, just as they need us to help them develop appropriate technology and a commerce which doesn't depend on wasteful packaging. And together we need the understanding, patience, and compassion to listen to each other, learn each other's needs, and share. In this, ordinary people like us have to lead the way.

The Divine Self

*A true votary of the Gita does not know what
disappointment is.*   – *Mahatma Gandhi*

IT IS OFTEN tempting to feel despair about
the environmental crisis. The changes in habit which we
all need to make, and the forces of insensitivity and self-
interest which prevent us from changing as quickly as
we should, can seem insurmountable.

But as you meditate more and more deeply, you will
find a rich source of hope and strength within. You will
make the discovery which the Bhagavad Gita and all
the great mystics promise, the discovery which fueled
Gandhi's extraordinary achievements: whatever selfishness is in our minds, whatever unkindness or insensitivity
to other creatures is in our life, is all merely a covering.
It is just a thick layer of conditioning that hides our real
goodness and kindness, which is the nature of the divine
Self who is in everyone.

If you remind yourself just once every day that there is
a source of unfailing kindness and unchanging love at the
core of your consciousness, it will help you. As you learn
to find it in yourself, you will simultaneously learn to see
it in others, and to help them find it themselves.

Reading the Mystics

WE ARE SO IMMERSED these days in what the mass media offer that it is helpful to give half an hour or so each day to reading the scriptures and the writings of the great mystics of all religions.

Their experiences and encouraging words can give us the support and companionship we need to keep up our efforts to transform our lives. Just before bedtime, after evening meditation, is a particularly good time for spiritual reading, because the thoughts you fall asleep in will be with you throughout the night.

Gentleness

Blessed are the meek, for they shall inherit the earth. — *Jesus, the Sermon on the Mount*

TO ME, the word "meek" here means "gentle." Gentleness is a quality conspicuous by its absence in our modern world. In order to be truly gentle you have to be secure and in order to be secure you have to be inwardly very strong.

When a great figure like Jesus speaks of gentleness, it is gentleness founded upon the rock of strength. People who get angry easily, who threaten you and spread scandals about you, have no toughness in them. Isn't Jesus called

"Gentle Jesus, meek and mild"? He can afford to be meek and mild because his strength comes entirely from within.

It's imperative for us to teach our children this because, for the most part, the media have given them models only of violence and anger, of people who threaten or are intimidated. To quote T. S. Eliot, such people are all stuffed with straw. They have nothing inside. As your spiritual awareness grows, you will find you have a very gentle fellow-feeling for all creatures, because you will be growing in inner strength. More and more, you will find that you are protecting all those around you.

A Healthy Profit

I DIFFER FROM SOME of those working to protect the environment in that I have no desire to injure or punish large corporations. On the contrary, I respect them, but I would like to see them freed from a good deal of the profit motive. Not all, of course, since a healthy profit motive is not a bad motivator, but when profit becomes the sole measure of success, a business runs the risk of harming not only its customers and the environment but also the spiritual well-being of its workers and owners.

Take certain parts of the chemical industry, for example. Today, even though it is clear that they destroy the earth's stratospheric ozone layer, chlorofluorocarbons and other ozone-destroying chemicals are being produced and used by several companies. There is little doubt that each pound of such chemicals we produce will contribute to skin cancers and will injure the ecosystem, yet "the bottom line" demands that they be produced as long as they are not banned.

This is what happens when the thirst for profit takes over, and it is what Jesus was talking about when he said that you can't love God and Mammon at the same time. You can't make profit your highest purpose and still say you love people. The Buddha would say that anyone who works in the manufacture or sales of ozone-destroying chemicals – or handguns or cigarettes or weapons of mass destruction – shares responsibility for the disease and damage they cause.

I believe that businesses, both big and small, have an important role to play in the health and well-being of our world. We need their tremendous corporate and managerial skills to restore the environment and contribute to society.

There is a long spiritual business tradition for modern business people to draw upon, going back as far as the wealthy merchant who endowed the Buddha with a magnificent park in which to train his disciples. When that merchant, not an ascetic but a wealthy man of the world, was asked what sort of person would emerge from the new forest university, he gave a reply that should be the motto inscribed over all our business schools: "Always a friend to all and always at work for all."

As my close friends know, I am not an "either-this-or-that" man. Let us have a healthy profit, but let us also remember that the real reason all of us have come into life is to give and give and give – not only until it hurts, but when it hurts, too.

Our children need to learn this from their earliest years, through the example of their parents and grandparents. Students need to learn this from their teachers, not only through their words, but through their personal life as well. We have been so conditioned to get and to take and to grab that we don't realize how healing it is to give. Physically, emotionally, intellectually, and spiritually, we can find our deepest, most lasting satisfaction in giving our time, our skills, our talent, our resources, to causes that benefit all.

As St. Francis would say (and he would find corroboration in modern heart research), It is in giving that we receive health, happiness, security, and strength. The more we give, the more we have. That is how a healthy profit is achieved. In fact, I have a suggestion for our business schools. Let us ask the graduates to acquire two M.B.A.'s – not just a Master of Business Administration but a Master of Bountiful Assistance as well.

Every Child Will Be Your Child

THE CHINESE CALL the universe by a picturesque name, "the ten thousand things," which stands for infinite multiplicity. To me, the wonder is not so much the vast variety of different forms of life, but the realization that the whole is not complete without the least of us. This is the awareness that we can develop through dedicated practice of meditation and the allied disciplines. In international politics, we become aware that the world is not complete without even a little country like the Maldives or Moldova; if its interests are left out, the world will be so much less. For that reason, I would say the idea of national planning is not enough. All our planning should be world planning – for politics, economics, education, and health.

This especially applies to the environment. If you are meditating well, you will begin to see that the world is not complete without every creature, even the smallest and seemingly most insignificant. You can confirm in your own experience what science is slowly discovering: that all forms of life are interconnected in countless invisible ways. As you become more and more aware of the Self, you will become aware of this daily relationship that you have with all people, all children, all animals, trees, rivers, and mountains. Every child will be your child; every forest will be your forest.

Mother Earth

The human race is a family. Men are brothers.
All wars are civil wars.   *– Adlai Stevenson*

IN HINDU MYSTICISM, the earth is always referred to as a very patient woman. She has to bear with all our misdeeds. We are all her children. Perhaps there is no greater sorrow for a mother than to see her children quarreling among themselves. In my village, two brothers quarreling or two sisters quarreling will be taken up as a village issue, since this is considered to be something that should never happen; it's no longer a domestic issue, but a community one.

The word for sibling in Sanskrit is *sahodara. Saha,* "together," *udara,* "womb": they come from the same womb. They have lived in the same womb. So they should always help each other. Similarly, we all come from the womb of Mother Earth. We are all brothers and sisters.

Just as a human mother is in agony when she sees her children fighting against one another, so Mother Earth is in agony when she sees nation fighting against nation, race against race. Through the enthusiastic practice of meditation and the allied disciplines, each of us can become instruments of peace and harmony, drawing upon our deepest resources to prevent nation from rising up against nation, race against race, brother against brother.

Peace is not created by governments and fighting forces. Peace is made by little people like you and me getting to know other people, other countries, other races. Invite them into your homes, ask them about their country, and you'll find what I discovered after coming to the U.S. over thirty years ago.

When I went back to visit India my relatives and friends asked me, "How did you find people there?"

"Just as I find people here," I said.

"Really?"

"Yes. They like everybody to be kind to them; they like everybody to be good to them; they like peace among people; they like loving relationships among people."

This is what people in every country are looking for. And after my talks in the early days in this country friends would ask me the same question, "How do you like it here?" I replied, "The same as I liked it there. You and I have ninety-nine percent in common and a delightful one percent not in common."

All the wars and exploitation, the inability to communicate, and the competition for resources that now plague the world derive from that one percent of difference. Every day, by our words and actions, each of us can be a gentle reminder to the world of all that we have in common.

Take a Chance on Kindness

All men should be willing to engage in the risk and the wager of ahimsa because violent policies have not only proved bankrupt but threaten man with extinction. – Thomas Merton

I'VE HEARD IT SAID that all of us have a little tendency to gamble, at least to take an occasional flutter. I like it when Merton says, in effect, "Hey! Why don't you bet on something that really pays?" Try to be kind to those who are unkind to you, and look upon it as a gamble. It will satisfy your gambling instinct and you won't have to waste money playing lotto.

Once, on my way to Berkeley, I read a big electronic sign posted at the race track near the freeway. "Win $10,000 next Saturday," it promised. The sun was shining in my eyes and I couldn't quite read the next line, which seemed to say, LOSING DAY. It was only on the way home that I read it properly, CLOSING DAY. The first impression was more accurate. For one person who wins $10,000, there are nine hundred and ninety-nine who go away sadder and, one would hope, wiser.

Similarly, often we are not quite sure how the other person is going to respond to our patience or our kindness. I am prepared to concede that you may get short shrift for awhile. They may even add insult to injury. That's the gamble. Double your bet. Isn't that the gambler's principle? You keep on doubling your bet until one day you redeem all your losses.

In the Gita, Sri Krishna says that even the gambler

trying to break the bank is not really looking for millions of dollars. He is looking to break into the bank within and come back loaded – with freedom from depression, freedom from resentment, freedom from hostility, and freedom from silly sense cravings. Rich relationships and a great capacity to contribute for the benefit of the world, that is the jackpot which everyone is looking for.

Peacemaking

I FIRST CAME TO the United States in 1959 by way of a P. & O. ocean liner, as part of the Fulbright exchange. On board were several other Fulbright scholars, including a few from countries whose relations with India were very strained. At the dining table they would take out their international frustrations on me as if I were the Prime Minister of India. I would plead innocence: "I am just a poor professor. What do I have to do with making important policies?" But my protests did little to stem the unpleasantness.

Quite a few of my Indian colleagues left the table to sit as far away as possible. I would have done the same before I had taken to meditation, but now I was secure. It is not that I did not understand the remarks. I understood them all too well, and I felt sad that neighboring countries should be indulging in such animosity. Yet it didn't really bother me except on their account. I simply didn't reply, but I didn't move away or become hostile either.

The surprise ending came when I got off at Marseilles.

These same hostile scholars came to see me. They were going on with the ship to Gibraltar and they had decided to give me a farewell party. I was amazed and a little embarrassed when they said, "Please forgive us for whatever we said."

This is the natural human response to patience and respect. It shows you the power of meditation. Good meditators do not bury their heads in the sand and say, "Everybody is good; everybody is loving." They know the world is a difficult place but they have enough security, endurance, and love to remember that all these difficulties are only on the surface of life. Beneath the anger and agitation runs the river of love.

So the test of wisdom is your capacity to be friendly in the midst of differences and secure in the midst of opposition. This can be true of nations also. Einstein made the understatement of his career when he said, "We know a few things that the politicians do not know." I like that statement very much. When we lead, the politicians follow. Often we do not lead, so they mislead us.

A House United

SURELY THERE IS NO spectacle more
tragic than the one described by Abraham Lincoln as "a
house divided against itself" – civil war. As I write this
book, dozens of countries are being torn asunder by it, with
untold cruelties being inflicted upon men, women, and
children. Many other countries are suffering from ethnic
and racial tensions that flare into violence between neighbor and neighbor, family and family. Even the "first world"
countries of America and Europe are not immune. In
our highly armed, high-tech world, such conflicts pose a
threat not just to our society, but to the earth and future
generations.

As discouraging as they can be, we should remember
that these are not clashes between armies but people, and
that the most powerful way to transform people is not
through violence or punishment or sanctions, but through
patient personal example. Every one of us has a role to play
in this great task, right in our own home and community. It
doesn't require speaking or writing or political skills. It
requires ideals and the desire to live by them. I can illustrate with an incident from my own life.

In the early days of my academic career, India was
undergoing the agony of civil war between Muslims and
Hindus. On the eve of the partition of Pakistan and India, I
was posted to a college in central India not far from the
University of Nagpur, where I had studied.

When I arrived on the campus, I went to the office and
signed my contract. I knew nobody there, nor did I know
the language, and I was wondering where on earth I would

stay. I headed outside to a horse carriage, which was waiting with my luggage. I planned to return to town and look for a room in a hotel.

As I climbed into the carriage, I was surprised to see one of my dearest Muslim friends from college running towards me. Naimuddin and I had attended postgraduate school together and had lived in the same dorm. A gracious and modest man, he was a much better scholar than I, at home in Urdu, Persian, Arabic, and Turkish, but when I praised his linguistic and research skills, he would simply say, "I rob dead men's graves. You've got the living touch. Don't ever lose it."

So he jumped into my horse carriage and told the driver to go to his home. I was puzzled. "You're coming with me," he said, "and you're going to stay with me." That was all.

We arrived at his residence, a big medieval mansion entrusted to him by a *Nawab,* a Muslim aristocrat, who had gone on pilgrimage to Mecca. I accepted his generous invitation and stayed.

But those were difficult, dangerous days for Hindus and Muslims. In some cities terrible violence had been unleashed, and on our campus the spirit of unity had received such a setback that Hindu and Muslim students used to sit on opposite sides of the classroom. Even the faculty was becoming polarized.

I should mention here that Naimuddin and I were not brave people. In fact, he was even less brave than I was, which is saying a good deal. But we had ideals, and we were prepared to stand by them. So we said, "Why shouldn't we stay together?" It was summer and we decided to sleep in the open, so that anybody who wanted to attack might get the chance. Many of my friends warned us, "You're both going to get hurt. Being idealistic is one thing, being practical is another." I disagreed then and I still disagree. Experience confirmed our faith in human nature. Not a single person caused us trouble.

Encouraged, Naimuddin and I undertook an experiment. In the evening, sitting together with a few other junior faculty members, Naimuddin would recite the *Rubaiyat of Omar Khayyam* in the beautiful Persian original. I would recite FitzGerald's excellent English translation. These great verses are irresistible to any poetry lover, and there were many poetry lovers in my classes, both Hindu and Muslim.

> Awake! for Morning in the Bowl of Night
> Has flung the Stone that puts the Stars to Flight:
> And Lo, the Hunter of the East has caught
> The Sultán's Turret in a Noose of Light.

It was only a matter of time before the news spread. One by one, students began to wander by and stand in the door, then step in, then sit down. Eventually, a good crowd of Hindus and Muslims were gathered there every Saturday, sitting side by side, listening together to the verses.

During our tenure at that college – even when tensions were very high – Naimuddin and I persevered. We shared the mansion. We walked to campus together. We recited poetry and staged plays together. And just because two people carried their ideals into practice, the atmosphere of the whole campus changed.

Last week I read about a terrible flood that swept away

thousands of people in Kashmir, on both the Indian and Pakistani sides. I was deeply touched to read how Indian and Pakistani soldiers – usually at odds – worked together to save lives and rescue cattle, forgetting past differences. In such events we glimpse the noblest part of human nature, our true personality. All the rest – the fighting, the retaliation, the vendettas – are nothing but a covering, a cloud of smoke obscuring our real Self.

It is my prayer that, through such cooperation, seemingly insignificant people like you and me will be able to dampen and eventually extinguish the fires of hatred which now trouble so many communities and countries – in the former Yugoslavia, in the poor countries of Africa, in the capitals of Europe, and in the inner cities of the United States. It doesn't take large numbers to change human relationships in any country, even today. It doesn't take government action. It takes dedication, determination, and a certain amount of faith in the goodness hidden in our hearts.

It takes you.

Afterword

IN THIS BOOK I have spoken quite a bit about ideals. To me, ideals are not vague, abstract concepts but living forces as real as gravity or electromagnetism. People who have the daring and determination to live out their ideals release a tremendous beneficial power into their lives, and that power will begin to transform the world they live in. Mahatma Gandhi called this "practical idealism," which means that it can be practiced in every aspect of life. It doesn't call so much for great acts of heroism as for a continuing, persistent effort to transform ill will into good will, self-interest into compassion.

For those who would like to explore this path of practical idealism, here are a few suggestions.

The Eight-Point Program of meditation and allied disciplines outlined in this book is the most powerful tool I know for establishing harmony in your life and releasing your deepest resources of creativity and compassion. To get started, review the eight points and begin practicing them right away:

Meditation, page 19
Repetition of the Mantram, page 32
Slowing Down, page 38
One-Pointed Attention, page 71
Training the Senses, page 68
Putting Others First, page 52
Spiritual Companionship, page 62
Reading the Mystics, page 110

If you would like more detailed instructions in these eight points, please see my book *Meditation*.

The recommendations in this book are, for the most part, quite simple. Yet it is often not easy to make the lifestyle changes they require. For this, meditation and the other spiritual disciplines – especially spiritual companionship – can give you much-needed support. There is a network of people following this Eight-Point Program who get together regularly and share spiritual companionship. The Blue Mountain Center of Meditation (Box 256, Tomales, California 94971) can provide you with more information.

The environmental crisis offers not only a challenge but an opportunity to transform the foundations of our society. In *The Compassionate Universe,* I have tried to detail the habits of thinking, feeling, and living which have contributed to our environmental crisis, and have offered suggestions about how we as individuals can find spiritual fulfillment.